COMEDY
CENTRAL:
The Essential Guide to

COMEDY

COMEDY

CENTRAL:

The Essential Guide to

COMEDY

Because There's a Fine Line
Between Clever and Stupid

BY CHRISTOPHER CLARO
AND JULIE KLAM

A Byron Preiss Visual Publications, Inc. Book

BOULEVARD BOOKS, NEW YORK

COMEDY CENTRAL: THE ESSENTIAL GUIDE TO COMEDY

A Boulevard Book/published by arrangement with
Byron Preiss Visual Publications, Inc.

PRINTING HISTORY
Boulevard trade paperback edition/April 1997

The Putnam Berkley World Wide Web site address is
http://www.berkley.com/berkley

ISBN: 1-57297-108-8

BOULEVARD
Boulevard Books are published by The Berkley Publishing Group,
200 Madison Avenue, New York, New York 10016.
BOULEVARD and its logo are trademarks
belonging to Berkley Publishing Corporation.

PRINTED IN THE UNITED STATES OF AMERICA

10 9 8 7 6 5 4 3 2 1

CONTENTS

CONTENTS

COMEDY CENTRAL:

The Essential Guide to

COMEDY

INTRODUCTION

We're only young once—but with humor, we can be immature forever.

—Art Gliwer

Options. Americans are faced with just too damn many of them. According to a recent survey, the average supermarket sells over forty varieties of mustard alone. There are too many books to read, too many movies to see, too many low fat granola bars to sample. And of course, there's just too damn much comedy: too many brick walls, too much "Hey, what's the deal with that airline food?," too much "Siskel and Ebert call it the funniest movie since *Chariots of Fire.*"

And it's because of this boom, for better or worse, that we bring you *Comedy Central: The Essential Guide to Comedy.* There's just so much stuff out there and so many places to find it that you need something to point to what's really worth your time.

- What are the comedies that are really worth renting in the video store? (Note: None of them takes place at a frat house, a ski lodge or a police precinct.)

1

- Which comics are doing more than just the "Hey, anybody here ever go to high school?" brand of standup?
- Which of the incessantly rerun television sitcoms are really the best?
- What about comedy albums? Which ones really endure?
- Are words with a *k* really funny?
- Which colleges are the funniest?
- What are the forbidden topics of standup comedy?

Comedy Central: The Essential Guide to Comedy isn't just a compass that points you toward the very best comedy available; it's also an exclusive backstage pass to the world of humor and the people who make it happen. *The Essential Guide to Comedy* is the book to turn to when you're at a loss. You want something funny, but you want to make sure that it doesn't involve a guy with a hammer and a melon or have the word *Academy* or *6* in the title. So forge on, dear reader, secure in the knowledge that *The Essential Guide to Comedy* is here to help you negotiate the ever-expanding minefield of comedy. Thanks for coming tonight. We'll be here all week. Please tip your waitress and try the veal.

WHERE
IS
COMEDY
CENTRAL?

The saving grace of humor: If you fail, at least you don't have anyone laughing at you.

—A. Whitney Brown

In 1989 HBO, owned by Time Warner, announced the launch of the Comedy Channel, a cable network devoted exclusively to comedy, twenty-four hours a day. Five days after the announcement of the Comedy Channel, Viacom, owner of MTV, Nickelodeon and Nick at Nite, announced the launch of HA! The TV Comedy Network. The pundits observed: "Two comedy networks owned by two media behemoths? It'll never work."

For once, the pundits were right on the money. At that time, cable television could only support one network for each specialized subject. CNN controlled the market for news. ESPN sated the public's desire for sports updates. And TNN was the one place to go for line dancing. This one-for-one ratio has begun to change with the current advent of competition from the likes of MSNBC, CNN/SI and The Redneck Bowling Network. However, comedy remains with only one specialized network. Why is this? Because

Comedy Central executives know a few "people," and it is probably for the best if you didn't ask any more questions.

The Comedy Channel was launched in November 1989 with a schedule of clips from comedy movies and TV specials. The network was hosted by a variety of comics and actors, including comedian Allan Havey, David Anthony Higgins of "Ellen," Steve Higgins, who has gone on to work as the head writer at "Saturday Night Live," and Nick Bakay, who worked on "In Living Color," Dennis Miller's short-lived late night talk show, and who also provided commentary for ESPN and now hosts Comedy Central's sports specials.

On April Fool's Day 1990, HA! The TV Comedy Network made its debut. The HA! schedule emulated that of Nick at Nite in that it consisted primarily of reruns of old television series. On any given day, a HA! viewer could feast on the likes of "Love, American Style," "Occasional Wife," "McHale's Navy" and "That Girl." The reruns were supplemented by some original series, which introduced such performers as Denis Leary, Jon Stewart and Brian O'Connor.

It was December 1990 when the two rival cable networks announced that they would become one. Rumors about such a merger had begun even before the launch of HA!, but an ongoing lawsuit between Viacom and Time Warner kept the principals from discussing a marriage of the two.

The two warring factions called a truce, merged their troops and regrouped to fight the war for viewers. Renamed (temporarily) CTV: The Comedy Network, the new entity used bits and pieces from both networks as programming.

Six months later, the network was renamed (permanently) Comedy Central. A bustling cartel full of people whose goal it is to generate gobs of laughs, Comedy Central is *the* home for all kinds of comedy. The network has evolved into its philosophy of "same world, different take," where it provides a skewed, funny perspective on the world and the things in it which you might normally take for granted.

For example, take "The Daily Show," created in 1996 by the producers of "The Jon Stewart Show." The show is hosted by Craig Kilborn, who gained legions of fans for his sarcastic and often hilarious remarks during sports highlights as an anchor at ESPN. At Comedy Central, Kilborn turns his wit on such targets as news, trends, pop culture, current events, politics, sports, and entertainment. An accurate reflection of Comedy Central's point-of-view, "The Daily Show" comments on the world through the perspective of a unique, knowing lens. All that *and* daily potshots at implausible celebrities like Michael Bolton and The Mommies!

While "The Daily Show" is quick and barbed, Comedy Central's "Dr. Katz, Professional Therapist" is quiet and low-key. In the animated series, Dr. Katz is given a voice by comedian Jonathan Katz, whose subdued delivery makes him a soothing balm to the insecure, neurotic comics who frequent his office.

Comedy Central introduced America to Patsy and Edina, the British booze-swilling fashion hounds of "Absolutely Fabulous." It was the original home of "Politically Incorrect with Bill Maher," where actors, musicians, writers and politicians spout off on anything from Bosnia to "Baywatch." And it's the place where you can see someone as beloved as

Bill Murray or as barely-tolerated as Englebert Humperdink attempt to answer "Craig's Five Questions."

Comedy Central has provided exposure for a number of stand-up comics as well. Bill Maher developed "Politically Incorrect" before bringing it to ABC. Tom Rhodes went to Vietnam for Comedy Central before he went into the classroom for NBC in "Mr. Rhodes." Jon Stewart worked as host of "Short Attention Span Theater" prior to hosting his talk show and appearing in feature films. Darrell Hammond went from starring in a Comedy Central–produced training video to working as a performer on "Saturday Night Live." Jim Breuer, also an SNL regular, got his first television exposure at Comedy Central.

And so, it's with this pedigree that we bring you *Comedy Central: The Essential Guide to Comedy*. As the comedy experts, we felt it was incumbent upon us to transfer our knowledge to the printed page. We've always thought books were really cool, from *Moby Dick* to *The Other Side of Midnight*, and we wanted to play in the publishing sandbox. But remember, the stuff in this book is just our opinion. These are our favorites and we wanted to turn readers on to them. It is by no means definitive . . . well, actually, it is definitive. This book is the comedy gospel according to the comedy experts. Amen.

A Brief History of Comedy

We are a nation that has always gone in for the loud laugh, the wow, the belly laugh and the dozen other labels for the roll-'em-in-the-aisles of gagerissimo.
—James Thurber

I f you were to ask Milton Berle, he'd tell you that there are only twelve basic jokes, and every bit you've ever heard is a variation on one or more of that magic dozen. Although Berle never actually identified the Big Twelve, you begin to suspect he was onto something when you look back at comedy that predates our great-grandparents. Granted, there are different styles of telling the jokes. And the subject matter of a comedian doing standup today is a lot more risqué than anything we would have heard in 1924. But it's amazing how familiar some of the old routines can sound.

It's possible that you could be watching something as contemporary as "Full House" or "Blossom" and hear a joke that sounds kind of familiar, and that could be because the joke's been around since the mid-nineteenth century. Like this one:

Who was that lady I saw you with last night?
That was no lady. That was my wife.

Back in the days of vaudeville (which lasted well into the 1920s), jokes like that one were considered surefire laugh-getters. Here are some other vaudeville gems you might recognize:

The baby swallowed my collar button last night.
Oh, you must have been very upset.
You bet I was. It was the only one I had.

My boy, when Abraham Lincoln was your age, he used to walk thirty miles to school every day.
Yeah, and when he was your age, he was President.

I spent two weeks in Philadelphia last Wednesday.

Now, it's true that there was smart, urbane humor around during the twenties that made these jokes hoary groaners even then. But the sophisticated stuff was really limited to two sources: books and the Broadway stage. On Broadway, playwrights like George S. Kaufman and Moss Hart created works that still make people laugh today. In print, Ring Lardner, Robert Benchley, Dorothy Parker and other *New Yorker* writers and spiritual descendants of Mark Twain demonstrated their searing wit.

Though an audience existed for smart, well-written material, when people went to a vaudeville house the last thing they wanted was a mental challenge. So what they saw on the stage tended to be baggy pants, floppy shoes and squirting seltzer bottles—and jokes like the ones just mentioned.

By the 1930s, vaudeville had been pushed aside by both talking movies and radio. But if you're interested in advances in comedy, don't listen to any old radio shows. Most radio comics (Fred Allen being a notable exception) simply took their vaudeville routines and performed them in front of a microphone. In fact, about the only innovation you're likely to find in a radio comedy of the thirties is a new topic for people to laugh at: the Great Depression. On a good night, listeners would hear Eddie Cantor or Jack Benny telling jokes like these:

Who was the fellow who jumped out the window on the twentieth floor?
He was some guy who was always getting in on the ground floor.

I met a guy who was out of work on the street the other day. He said he hadn't had a bite in three days. So I bit him.

The thirties, however, are also known as the era of the sophisticated movie comedy. Movies then relied less on gag lines than on character development and zany situations. They were in the tradition of the best of Broadway and had nothing to do with vaudeville. If you want to check out the top movie products of this era, head down to the video store and start with copies of *My Man Godfrey, It Happened One Night* and *The Front Page.*

As for the 1940s, it's probably best to split the decade in

THE ADVENTURES OF ABBOT AND COSTELLO

Abbot and Costello Go to Mars

Abbot and Costello in Hollywood

Abbot and Costello in the Foreign Legion

Abbot and Costello Meet Captain Kidd

Abbot and Costello Meet Dr. Jekyll and Mr. Hyde

Abbot and Costello Meet Frankenstein

Abbot and Costello Meet the Invisible Man

Abbot and Costello Meet the Keystone Kops

Abbot and Costello Meet the Killer

Abbot and Costello Meet the Mummy

---

half. During the first five years, comedy—along with just about everything else in American life—was pretty much frozen in place while the country took care of some trouble in Europe and the Pacific. Without question, the high point of forties comedy is the perfectly structured, exquisitely timed Abbott and Costello bit "Who's on First?" It's been called one of the best pieces of comedy ever devised, and that evaluation is hard to argue with. It was a product, however, not of the forties, but of the 1920s. Abbott and Costello learned the basic routine during their vaudeville days in the early thirties, and it was a staple even then. What they did was expand it, sharpen it and—most important—per-

THE LEAST FUNNY RADIO SHOWS OF ALL TIME

Fibber McGee & Molly

Duffy's Tavern

Amos & Andy

The Jack Benny Show

Imus in the Morning

form it on radio and film, where it was recorded and passed down to us.

The second half of the forties, however, did offer some new developments. Its true that much of the tired old material still dominated the menu in the celebrated Borscht Belt, the string of Jewish resorts in the Catskill Mountains of upstate New York. But some of the younger comics broke out of the belt and opened doors that would lead to a real revolution in the next decade. Sid Caesar and Carl Reiner took their Catskills material (and a young writer named Mel Brooks) to the brand-new medium of television and began creating baggy-pants shtick that came very close to actual satire.

That satire became the hallmark of fifties television comedy, most notably on "Your Show of Shows." This was a live, ninety-minute comedy/variety show aired on Saturday nights, hosted by Caesar. Many of the sketches on the show were lampoons of contemporary movies and were the forerunners of the kind of comedy that would later be performed on "The Carol Burnett Show" and "Saturday Night Live."

The writer's room at "Your Show of Shows" is legendary because of the astonishing list of people who started there. In addition to Carl Reiner and Mel Brooks, Larry Gelbart, Neil Simon and Woody Allen all served time writing for Caesar.

While Caesar's show was essentially a revue performed on television, Steve Allen's comedy involved playing around with the medium itself. As the first host of "The Tonight Show," Allen brought his cameras out on to the streets of New York to find comedy. He broke out of the confines of the studio to perform stunts like being lowered into a huge vat of Jell-O. (If some of the things Allen tried sound familiar, it's because David Letterman, who has always acknowledged Steve Allen's influence on his career, has emulated a lot of them on his late night shows.)

In the late fifties and early sixties, television comedy was given another jolt by a comic named Ernie Kovacs. Kovacs used the television as if it was a plaything in his rec room. His grasp of the mechanics of television informed everything he did on the air. He used effects and technology to enhance his comedy, such as wiping images off the screen and superimposing a woman's face over a man's body. He produced a half-hour silent program with tilted sets on which the cameras were skewed to the same angle as the sets, so everything appeared to be level. But when Kovacs's character, Eugene, tried to pour milk or eat an olive, the incline affected the action. Kovacs's techniques were later copied by the producers of such series as "Laugh In" and "The Electric Company."

At the same time that Kovacs was changing television in the early sixties, standup comedy was also evolving. Instead of doing generic material ("Just got back from a pleasure trip. Took my mother-in-law to the airport."), comics like Woody Allen, Lenny Bruce and Bill Cosby were taking their life experience and turning it into comedy.

Lenny Bruce has become famous for his fights with the law and his death by drug overdose. But his standup comedy—prior to the period during which he did nothing but read court transcripts—was truly exceptional. He was equally adept at straight movie parodies—playing the warden, the convict and the priest during a prison break—as he was at calling attention to issues of race that Americans began to deal with in the early sixties. He combined elements of vaudeville with the sensibility of a guy who had grown up around the hippest of jazz musicians.

Cosby, on the other hand, started as a kid from Philadelphia whose standup was about a kid from Philadelphia. He spun epic tales of go-cart races, snowball fights and tonsillectomies. He was raised on radio, and it showed in the way he could hold an audience with nothing but a microphone.

Cosby was immensely popular across the country. He played the Playboy Club and Mr. Kelly's in Chicago, the big showrooms of Las Vegas and the concert halls in New York and San Francisco. The universality of his material

made it resonate with many different audiences, and, from his earliest appearance, he exuded a confidence onstage that the audience warmed up to. As Phil Berger said about Cosby in his book, *The Last Laugh*: "No beginner's kinks in his style. He was the flimflam man from the start."

One of his best bits was "Chicken Heart," a sendup of the "Inner Sanctum" radio show that Cosby and his brother, Russell, listened to as children. The brilliant thing about the routine was the way Cosby made it accessible to every member of the audience, even those who weren't old enough to remember old-time radio.

When he went to work for producer Sheldon Leonard on "I Spy," in the mid-1960s, Cosby's stories about television production and international travel worked as well as his earlier routines about his childhood. No matter what was going on in his life, audiences could relate to it. That was one of the things that made his standup comedy successful.

After "I Spy," Cosby continued to make a solid living in nightclubs, concert halls and casinos. But repeating his television success was difficult. He starred in no fewer than three failed series between 1969 and 1984, before he finally had a hit with "The Cosby Show."

"The Cosby Show" was a natural outgrowth of Cosby's standup material: two loving, successful parents raising their four children. Cosby's character was little more than a variation on the many sorely tried sitcom fathers who had come before him, but he infused the role with a sense that he had in real life endured the trials that his television kids put him through. The fact that he had experienced many of the situations depicted on the series gave it the same kind of universal appeal for audiences that his standup had.

Cosby's success as a standup in the early sixties opened the door for other black comics, many of whom had been relegated to playing smaller rooms and non-white audiences. Two of those who benefited from Cosby's success were Richard Pryor and Flip Wilson.

Flip Wilson was a young standup comic from St. Louis whose material owed a debt to Cosby in that it was essentially color-blind and therefore unthreatening to white audiences. Wilson entertained audiences with the shaggiest of shaggy dog stories, often taking listeners off on tangents, but always returning them to stories that had been around since before vaudeville. For example, there is the woman on the train with the baby whose seatmate goes on and on about just how ugly her child is. When she calls the conductor over to complain, he tells her "we'll get you another seat and we'll even get a banana for your monkey."

Wilson took his wide appeal to television in the late sixties and early seventies with his own variety show. Shrewdly produced to appeal to the broadest demographics possible, the show mixed Wilson's storytelling and sketch-performing with guests as varied as George Carlin, Bing Crosby, Perry Como and Richard Pryor.

Pryor arrived in New York in 1963, performing a kind

THE FORBIDDEN TOPICS OF STANDUP COMEDY

None

of comedy totally unlike the brand for which he would become famous. His early material showed none of the anger, or insight, of the routines he performed in his now-classic concert films. About those times, Pryor was quoted in Mel Watkins's book, *On the Real Side*, as saying "I made a lot of money being Bill Cosby."

But in the early 1970s, after a series of incidents that Pryor would later describe as indicative of a nervous breakdown, the comedian's true personality began to emerge onstage. What came out was a series of wicked, funny and vicious observations about the state of race relations in America.

Throughout the seventies, Pryor was an astute, caustic social commentator. He spoke to black audiences about their collective experience, and he made white crowds understand that experience.

Pryor's early New York performing experience coincided with that of a young comic named Woody Allen. He started, along with Neil Simon and Mel Brooks, as a writer for Sid Caesar on "Your Show of Shows." In the sixties, Allen began doing standup comedy. Where Cosby's early work played up the fun of being a kid, Allen's darkly humorous material focused on his seemingly endless list of neuroses. His stories were shot through with bad dates, neighborhood thugs and lousy parents. He couldn't even get a break from his analysts, strict Freudians all: *"If you kill yourself, they make you pay for the sessions you miss."*

Allen was the first standup to transfer his stage persona successfully to film. In fact, *Take the Money and Run*, Allen's first movie, actually contained lines that were lifted, intact, from his standup act.

As Cosby, Allen, Bruce and others were injecting intelligence into standup comedy, sixties television comedy seemed to be stuck at a second-grade level: genies living in bottles, nose-twitching witches and seven stranded castaways. Why? One theory was that there was so much turmoil in the world that television should be an escape from real life. Another theory held that network executives were

simply giving the public what they thought the public wanted. Many executives still hold to the latter theory.

In the seventies, television comedy began to show signs that someone was thinking. Instead of gimmicks, producers began to present intelligent characters and compelling situations. All of a sudden, TV comedy was *about* something.

"All in the Family" was the

first comedy show to challenge its audience, almost daring viewers to laugh at it. It had an audacity that was shocking for the period in which it aired. Concurrent with its popularity, a new permissiveness was being exercised by standup comics, George Carlin and Richard Pryor foremost among them.

George Carlin underwent a transformation, physical and otherwise, that began around 1968. His material up to that time consisted primarily of harmless impressions and TV parodies. In the late sixties he began to grow his hair, stop wearing suits onstage and, most importantly, discard his tame older material in favor of stuff for which he felt some passion.

Carlin would later say in an interview that, up until this change began to occur, he was playing to the parents of the people he really wanted to reach. When he realized he wanted to play to people his own age, he made a conscious effort to reach them. In doing so, he used language that had never been used in the main showrooms in Las Vegas, where his earlier material had been very successful.

Carlin was arrested on more than one occasion for violating local obscenity laws. It was this characteristic that most often drew comparisons to Lenny Bruce. Besides being a major part of his act, profanity also crafted his comedy. It was a tool. It just so happened that, like radar detectors, the tool was outlawed in many parts of the country.

Carlin's popularity surged in the seventies, but it never matched that of his contemporary, Richard Pryor, who, along with Steve Martin, gave rise to the phenomenon of "comedian as rock star."

Pryor was the first black standup comic to achieve real success in films. Throughout the seventies, he supplemented his standup work by acting in movies like *Silver Streak, Car Wash* and *Stir Crazy.* His concert films were among the first of their kind for a comic.

Inevitably, as his popularity grew, Pryor's connection to his audience diminished. He was no longer a poor kid from Peoria working the crowd. He was a movie star with a bad drug problem whose third concert film was devoted almost exclusively to a horrible freebasing accident that left 80 percent of his body burned. The audience couldn't relate to the experiences of a movie star. Pryor had become too big for standup comedy.

By the late seventies, Steve Martin was in danger of suffering a similar fate. His first album, "Let's Get Small," was released in 1976, just prior to his first "Saturday Night Live" appearance. Recorded in a small club in Los Angeles, it was vintage Steve Martin. His act was based primarily on the cheesy, white-suited lounge lizard he played onstage. He made balloon animals. He played the banjo. He sent up every hoary showbiz convention he experienced growing up near Disneyland.

But just as he began to make it as a standup, Martin almost became a victim of his own success. His second album, "A Wild & Crazy Guy" released in 1978, was recorded at the Universal Amphitheater in Los Angeles. Instead of the intimate feeling of the first album—just a guy doing his act for a crowd in a bar—the second was basically a rock concert. The crowd responded to Martin not with laughter but with loud cheering and hoots of recognition at his material. He had become an icon.

Martin used films as a way of getting out of standup. He recognized the need for a link to the audience and realized that the bigger he got, the less likely he would be to establish that link. So he became a movie star.

Beginning with *The Jerk* in 1979, Martin became the biggest standup to make it in movies since Pryor. He has said in interviews that he used standup as a means to an end—to make it in movies.

This was also the course Albert Brooks charted. Brooks had been doing standup comedy since the mid-sixties, appearing regularly on "The Ed Sullivan Show" and "The Tonight Show." He was widely acknowledged as one of the smartest standup comics in the business. He released two comedy albums in the seventies that remain two of the most innovative pieces of comedy ever produced.

"Comedy Minus One" had a side and a half of regular standup material. But it was Albert Brooks standup material, so it was amazing. At the end of side two (we're talking vinyl, this is almost twenty years ago), was an old vaudeville routine about taking a car into the mechanic. Brooks had a script printed inside the jacket of the album and recorded the bit with Georgie Jessel, as the car's owner, doing the setups. But he left out the mechanic's punch lines. Those were to be performed by the album's owner, using the printed script.

"A Star is Bought," Brooks's next album, contained a variety of pieces, each of which could be played by a radio station with a particular format. Brooks offered talk stations a mock call-in show where he not only took the calls, he made them. For classical stations, there was a version of "Bolero," with newly-discovered lyrics. And nostalgia stations could play an episode of "The Albert Brooks Show" from 1943, costarring Pat Carroll and Sheldon Leonard.

In the late seventies, Brooks put aside standup comedy and concentrated on making movies, which for him were intensely personal. In fact, he actually raised much of the production money for his first three films himself. Working as writer, director and star, he released his first film, *Real Life*, in 1979. It was the story of a vain, obnoxious film director named Albert Brooks who invades the home of a Phoenix family, planning to spend a year with them to document their daily lives.

As personal as Brooks's films have always been, none has ever been very successful at the box office. While he was making his small, personal works, the original cast members of "Saturday Night Live," a late night TV show that featured Brooks's short films during its first season in 1975, welcomed the eighties by leaving the late night show and going west to make movies.

It was the success of *National Lampoon's Animal House* in 1978 that made Hollywood realize that "Saturday Night Live" could be used as a farm team for film comedians. The most successful comedies of the 1980s each had at least one former member of the cast of "Saturday Night Live."

The "Saturday Night Live" sensibility stormed into movies like a group of pub-bound frat boys after midterms. Antiestablishment comedies like *Meatballs* and *Stripes* were huge hits. *Ghostbusters* combined wise-ass SNL humor with bogeymen and made millions. And in 1982, the biggest SNL star of all would make his movie debut.

Eddie Murphy had been a cast member of "Saturday Night Live" for a year and a half when he co-starred with Nick Nolte in *48HRS*. The movie was a huge hit and

THE WORST MOVIES MADE BY CURRENT OR FORMER CAST MEMBERS OF "SATURDAY NIGHT LIVE"

Oh, Heavenly Dog. Chevy Chase co-stars with Benji. Enough said.

Trapped in Paradise. Dana Carvey, Jon Lovitz and Nicolas Cage as brothers?

Feds. Mary Gross (remember her?) and Rebecca DeMornay study to become FBI agents. It's like an unfunny *Police Academy 7.*

Perfect. John Travolta and Jamie Lee Curtis you remember, but what about the waiflike and cadaverous Laraine Newman?

Clean Slate. Dana Carvey as a detective who loses his memory whenever he goes to sleep. This would have been really good if *Groundhog Day* hadn't come out a year earlier.

Billy Madison. Adam Sandler as a guy who has to go back to elementary school. A paean to morons everywhere.

Continental Divide. John Belushi falls in love with Blair Brown. We hear there's a remake in the works starring Pauly Shore and Sigourney Weaver.

Dead Heat. In the Joe Piscopo oeuvre, this movie is almost as good as his commercials for protein powder.

Murphy went from "that guy on 'Saturday Night Live,'" to a bona fide movie star.

Like his idol, Richard Pryor, Murphy combined standup comedy with film work. Also like Pryor, profanity was a large part of Murphy's act. And in a further parallel, Murphy was largely forced to stop doing comedy when his movie star persona separated him from his audience. Not everyone could relate to his stories about keeping your entourage from driving his Porsche to pick up the new leathers at the cleaners.

Still, throughout the eighties Murphy's films were huge hits. The first two installments of the *Beverly Hills Cop* series made over two hundred million dollars. His concert film, *Raw*, while criticized for Murphy's comments about gay men, was a big draw. And his specials for HBO always got big ratings for the cable network.

Some of Murphy's luster began to tarnish in the late eighties, as he modeled himself more and more on another of his idols, Elvis Presley. Surrounded by hangers-on in a walled-in New Jersey estate dubbed "Bubble Hill," Murphy began to believe his own press. He tried his hand at directing and created *Harlem Nights*, a film Roger Ebert reviewed by saying "[Murphy] approaches his story more as a costume party in which everybody gets to look great while fumbling through a plot that has not been fresh since at least 1938."

Harlem Nights was a harbinger of things to come for Murphy. Flaccid sequels like *Another 48HRS.* and *Beverly Hills Cop III* failed to draw the audiences his earlier work had. But in the early nineties, with the relative flops *Boomerang* and *The Distinguished Gentleman* behind him, Murphy claimed that he was going to keep at it until he hit again. And he may have reversed the slide with his impressive remake of Jerry Lewis's *The Nutty Professor*.

As Murphy's star was rising in the movies in the eighties, standup comedy was beginning to explode. Cable television had provided an outlet for hundreds of standup comics, the best of whom were snatched up by premium networks like HBO and Showtime and given their own specials. "It's Garry Shandling's Show" premiered on Showtime in 1986.

AND EVEN MORE OF THE WORST MOVIES MADE BY SNL CAST MEMBERS

Nothing But Trouble. With Dan Aykroyd and Chevy Chase, Leonard Maltin called it "stupefyingly unwatchable."

Spies Like Us. Chevy Chase and Dan Aykroyd go to the Middle East as spies. The camels in the movie have all the best lines.

Caddyshack II. They couldn't get Rodney Dangerfield, so they got Jackie Mason. They couldn't get Bill Murray, so they got Dan Aykroyd. But Chevy Chase? He's always up for sequel duty (see also *National Lampoon's European Vacation, Fletch Lives, National Lampoon's Christmas Vacation*).

Best Defense. When you make a comedy about the military, aren't the first two names you think of Eddie Murphy and Dudley Moore?

Johnny B. Goode. One-season cast members Anthony Michael Hall and Robert Downey, Jr. in a comedy about college football recruiting violations. Boy, those SNL people could find laughs in almost anything.

Haunted Honeymoon. Gilda Radner didn't live long enough to make more than a few really bad movies and this is the worst of them.

Cops and Robbersons. Jack Palance is a cop who has to commandeer the house of regular Joe, Chevy Chase, for a stakeout. It was the roaring success of this film and *Memoirs of an Invisible Man* that got Chase the nod over many Hollywood A-listers to star in *Man of the House.*

Shandling, who had started in show business as a writer for such series as "Welcome Back, Kotter" and "Sanford and Son," had established himself as a standup comic via his appearances on "The Tonight Show." He pitched his series, about the home life of a comic named Garry Shandling, to NBC. When they turned it down, he took it to Showtime.

The success of Shandling's show (which later was shown in week-delayed reruns on Fox) really opened the floodgates for standup comics to become sitcom stars. The networks began to recognize the potential of standup comics as ratings-getters and in 1988, Roseanne (nee Barr, nee Arnold) began working on a series for ABC. The series, based on Roseanne's self-proclaimed "domestic goddess" persona, was an instant hit.

Suddenly, the comedy business became The Business of Comedy, as the combination of home video, cable television and big budget movies took a bunch of comedians just telling jokes and turned them into an industry that would make millions of dollars in business yearly.

One of the by-products of the comedy boom was the rise of performers who did comedy, but were not comedians, per se. The first in this genre to come to prominence, thanks to an HBO special produced by Mike Nichols, was Whoopi Goldberg. She performed onstage, alone, but in character, addressing the audience as anything from a Valley girl to a junkie on the streets of New York.

When Eric Bogosian created his stage productions of "Sex, Drugs, Rock and Roll" and "Talk Radio," he challenged the audience in much the same way. He was onstage, wearing only black jeans and a white shirt, and he dared viewers to see him as a well-to-do suburbanite or a vitriolic radio talk-show host.

Bogosian and Goldberg were the members of the vanguard of solo, non-standup performers. As the nineties approached, many standup comics began to claim that their stage shtick was now a "one-man show," and the field became crowded with poseurs. Among those whose work was really unique, though, were Rick Reynolds, John Leguizamo and Danny Hoch.

The boom in comedy also resulted in a real estate glut. All of a sudden, every city, no matter how small and formerly unfunny, had a Chuckle Hut, a Ha Ha's, a Sir Laffs-A-Lot or an Improv. Comedy clubs are second only to Gap stores as the predominant use of most of the undeveloped real estate in the United States. It was virtually impossible to channel-surf without tripping over a comic in front of a brick wall telling us about the differences between New York and L.A. Or wondering how Jack Nicholson would be different if he worked at a Taco Bell.

Network executives, dazzled by the success of Roseanne's show, were soliciting comics and handing out pilot deals like they were Hershey bars on Halloween. NBC struck it rich with Jerry Seinfeld and made a hit of Paul Reiser's "Mad About You." ABC hit the comedy lottery with Tim Allen's "Home Improvement" and Ellen DeGeneres's show. And Shandling has done it again with "The Larry Sanders Show."

Comedy as a career is now being considered by people who once might have been lawyers or pharmacists. There's even comedy via computer, thanks to a CD-ROM starring the Monty Python troupe and countless sites on the World Wide Web.

So that's it. Comedy to date. There's more of it today than ever before. It's gone from being just a few comedians telling jokes to an industry that rivals General Motors. Is bigger better? The way we see it, the more funny out there, the better. In closing this chapter, we'll leave you with one thought from comic and former Hollywood Square, George Gobel:

"You can lead a horse to water—but before you push him in, just stop and think how a wet horse smells."

OPEN MIKERS: JEFF ROSS

It's kind of silly to heckle. You've spent big money to see the show, and you're ruining it for yourself. It's like going to the ballet and trying to trip the dancers.

—Jimmy Brogan

Open Mike Night. The very phrase has always represented one of the things that's really right about the comedy business. Anybody, from any profession, can walk in off the street and tell jokes to a crowd. The tellers can be terrible; they often are. Usually, the guy who takes his friend's advice to perform at an open mike is the last person who belongs there.

But what about the ones who aren't terrible? The people who get up there, and, even if they fail their first time out, realize that this is what they were meant to do. The ones who go back, night after night, working on the same five minutes of material; crafting it, honing it, sharpening it. Keeping what works and scrapping what doesn't. Learning how to work a crowd, how to hold a mike, how to hide flop sweat. How to be a pro.

It's those people that these spotlights profile; comics you probably don't know now. But wait. Follow them over the next year or two and we guarantee that they will become more than a little familiar to you. They were chosen not only because of their talent, but because we believe that they represent the next wave in standup comedy.

So, here for you to enjoy, is the first segment of Open Mike Night.

OPEN MIKERS: JEFF ROSS

Jeff Ross is a New Jersey boy who spent his adolescence as a combination cook/parking valet/ fruit cup assembler for his father's kosher catering business. The major requirement for making fruit cups? "You had to not mind the maraschino cherry crap all on your hands. I had red fingers from the age of fourteen to eighteen."

Boston University was seeking freshmen with fruit cup experience, so Jeff answered the call, majoring in communications with a minor in political science. When he graduated, he wrote and edited industrial films with a friend from college.

Jeff began doing standup but still worked his day job, which he valued as a source of jokes for his act. "As soon as comics stop working during the day, we lose a big part of our material. You have to have a life outside comedy, because it's hard to write jokes about writing jokes. When you're working, you can write jokes about your job, your boss, your paycheck. But once you become a working comic, you find yourself writing jokes about TV, lying around all day, drinking, airplanes."

To listen to Jeff is to hear a guy who knows that what he does is a job, and, like most jobs, some days it's great and others, it sucks. "I enjoy it when it goes well and when it doesn't go well, I want to jump out the window."

As with the practitioner of any craft, Jeff wants to put his best stuff out there for audiences, but always makes sure he has a backup. "When I was getting started, even if I wasn't getting laughs with jokes, I still got the audience to like me. But that's really not good enough. You always have to have a Plan B." After working as a comic for five years, Jeff can be brutally honest about his work: "I probably bombed my first seven or eight hundred times onstage. I finally had my first good set a couple of days ago. I guess that's why you guys called me for this book. You probably heard about it."

What we did hear about was one of Jeff's more far-flung gigs. "I played the University of Alaska, Fairbanks recently. I did a 7:30 show for the kids who couldn't drink, then a 10:00 for the ones who could. It was light out the entire time I was there. It took three planes to get there. I was exhausted. Couldn't move my bowels for a week." For all the wear and tear, though, the gig paid off. "You get out to Alaska and you can't help but kill. You don't fly to another planet and not do well. The kids were just so glad to see *somebody*."

As his standup career has become stronger, Jeff has made sure that his material has evolved as well, honing strong bits, but not hesitating to discard jokes, even stuff that may still work. "Sometimes young comics tell me 'I have this bit that I close with every time. I don't know what I would do without it.' I say 'I guarantee, in a year, you'll be embarrassed by it.' It happened to me. I remember I had this 'I've fallen, and I can't get up' joke. And I said 'I'm going to every club in town and if I open with that joke, I'll hook the audience.' You couldn't tie me to a stage right now and ask me to do that joke. I'd be too embarrassed."

When asked about his comedy role models, Jeff has a decidedly unhip response: "Don Rickles is my favorite. He is a comedian's comedian. He's the captain of politically incorrect, F.U. humor."

Jeff has one other comedy idol: "My grandfather. He was a pisser. Real, real dry. A lot like Rickles, but sometimes more clever. He would save it all up and let the zinger go when the time was right. I think that he made me the way I am."

As important as his grandfather was to Jeff, so were his parents, neither of whom lived to see him perform onstage. "It breaks my heart. My father used to love to go to Atlantic City and I won the TropWorld Comedy Competition there a few years ago. I got a lot of work out of it and it really got me out of the day job situation. It would have been nice if he'd been around for that."

Even with all his experience, Jeff is far from jaded. "Before I did my first TV shot, I said that if I ever did it on TV, I wouldn't care if I ever did it again, because it was such an amazing thing. Because that's really taking it pretty far, if someone's going to pay you to tell five minutes of jokes on television."

The awe that Jeff feels toward comedy is an attitude that permeates his work. "I used to think that comedy wasn't a very high calling. But over the years, people would stop me after the show and say things like 'My husband's very sick and I haven't seen him laugh like that in months.' You never know why someone's in a comedy club. Sometimes people are there for cheering up, or to escape for an hour and a half."

Those are the kinds of experiences that can help a comic gain a certain measure of confidence about himself. Of course, confidence is a hard thing to achieve in a business notorious for intense competition for the few spots that exist on television and in nightclubs. "I just did a reading of a play that I'm writing and a friend called me up to congratulate me. And the call went from 'I heard you did great' to 'If anybody should be writing a one-man show, it should be me, because . . . ' As much as you want to be happy for your friends, it's hard."

If confidence is hard, motivation is even harder. "I'm always going to make money in this business. I'm at a point where I feel like, without even trying, I could make a living if I just did the same jokes." While that can be a comforting notion, Jeff is concerned because it breeds laziness. "If you have a good 45-minute show, you can fall back on it for at least five years. But the motivation is really that you want to be able to look at yourself in the mirror. You want to be honest with yourself and be proud of yourself. And if you want to do that, you have to make your own opportunities. I don't want to be 45-years-old and waiting to audition for the next Albert Brooks movie. I want to be Albert Brooks."

He's also creating a one-man show that Jeff says will only

be slightly different from his standup. "I'm trying to make it as natural and relaxed as my act. But I don't feel like I need to have a laugh every thirty seconds. There'll be some tender moments, I hope. And I'm hoping people come away knowing me just a little better."

Jeff is philosophical about the breadth of opportunities available to him and others in the standup business. "Everybody gets their shot. If you're funny, you'll get it." Does he know funny people who haven't gotten their chance? "Yeah," Jeff says, "me."

Do You Have Anything with Richard Benjamin? or Movies! Movies! Movies!

When you do comedy (versus drama), you feel you're not eating at the adult table.

—Jerry Seinfeld

What separates comedy movies from comedy television shows is plainly the investment factor. Television, once you own a set, is free (unless you have cable, then it could run you about $29.95 a month, and if you have premium channels, forget about it.) But mostly, it's pretty cheap. Movie prices, however, rival that of compact cars. That's why you need to make your choice wisely. You can either wait to hear about comedy films from friends and colleagues or see how many Popcorns your local TV reviewer gives them. Because we all know that it's far more disappointing to see a comedy flop than a drama flop. What's going to happen if you see a bad drama? You don't get depressed enough? But, if you're all geared up for laughs, and you sit stone-faced for ninety minutes, man, that's bad! It may even be damaging, medically.

What we're saying is you need a list of guaranteed best comedy films. We know you have *your* favorites, but you've seen them already, and anyway, no one's going to pay us for that. We feel confident that our list will serve you better than any other because, over the years, we've seen every comedy movie—silent, foreign, even that one of your second birthday party when you cry at the clown. And, we've kept detailed movie logs in preparation for this very chapter.

Because you may not trust our judgment alone, we conducted extensive, grant-funded research, testing our list on amateur and professional moviegoers. We monitored them with small, electronic suction-like devices, and recorded their reactions. Responses such as "Hey where's the exit?" were ignored. What we found will surprise you. The list we started with was the very same list we ended up with.

This index isn't an indiscriminate jumble. It is a discriminating jumble organized into a single category: comedy movies every expert must see and undeservedly lesser known comedic gems that you must see. From here on in, you have no excuse.

DUCK SOUP (1933, B&W)

Everyone has to see a Marx Brothers movie, because one day someone will say to you "What's your favorite Marx brothers movie?" and you will not want to reply "I've never seen any." For this reason, and because it's a great film, you will want to see *Duck Soup*, unquestionably the best of the early Marx Brothers movies.

Unencumbered by too many big production numbers, *Duck Soup* is the story of a wealthy dowager who will give $20 million to the impoverished country of Fredonia if it

will make Rufus T. Firefly (Groucho Marx) its despot. Fire-fly romantically pursues Mrs. Teasdale, who is also the object of affection for Trentino (Louis Calhern) of neighboring Sylvania, who only wants Mrs. Teasdale to gain Fredonia for himself. Trentino then acquires the services of Vera Marcal (Raquel Torres) to seduce Firefly away, as well as Chicolino (Chico Marx), a peanut vendor, and Brownie (Harpo Marx) to sleuth. Eventually war breaks out, and here the plot gets really hard to follow.

Duck Soup includes the great mirror mime scene (remember when Lucy and Harpo reprised it on "I Love Lucy?") and is also the movie Woody Allen walks into in the happy flashback at the end of *Hannah and Her Sisters* (Hi-dee-hi-

45

THE MARX BROTHER'S REAL FIRST NAMES

Chico—Leonard

Groucho—Julius

Gummo—Milton

Harpo—Adolph

Zeppo—Herbert

---

dee-hi-dee-hi-dee-hi-dee-hi-dee-ho). See, you have a little party trivia already.

A flop with the critics and a slug at the box office, *Duck Soup* was the first real anti-war comedy. Before there was "M*A*S*H" and *Dr. Strangelove*, there was *Duck Soup*—a movie quite ahead of its time. Back then, nobody thought of making fun of war, at least not on film.

Duck Soup has historical significance as well. It was banned in Italy by Benito Mussolini for the movie's derogatory portrayal of Chicolini, the fictional dictator. Oddly enough, it was on Francisco Franco's Year's Ten Best list.

BROADWAY DANNY ROSE (1984, B&W)

Broadway Danny Rose is probably the only Woody Allen film that didn't inspire thousands of Topekans to move to New York. Essentially, it's a reminiscence about the career of Danny Rose (Woody Allen), a Sad Sack theatrical manager who handles one-armed jugglers, balloon folders and penguins dressed as rabbis. The storytellers are a collection of the old master comics (Corbett Monica, Morty Gunty, Sandy Baron, Howard Storm and Jackie Gayle) who hold court at a table in the Carnegie Deli. (Also present is Jack Rollins, Woody's real-life manager and producer.)

The dominant story revolves around Rose's one-time client Lou Canova (Nick "Apollo" Forte), a fifties greaser-type lounge singer whose biggest hit is the signature melody "Agita." When the married Canova has to do a big show, he asks Rose to act as a "beard" (fake boyfriend), and escort his girlfriend Tina (an almost unrecognizable Mia Farrow), a mobbed-up decorator with a weakness for animal prints. From a mistaken identification, a wild chase follows, giving much room for anxiety Allen style. One of the best moments comes when Tina and Danny Rose are being chased by mob pals of her boyfriend, because they think she and Danny are having an affair. Tina spots them and tells Danny to move or "They'll tear the tongue right out of your head." Danny responds incredulously, "What are you talking about? I'm just the beard. They'll tear the tongue out of the beard?"

Broadway Danny Rose plays like a standup routine. It is here that old Woody the comedian comes through, even using comics to tell the story of broad, over-the-top characters. *Broadway Danny Rose* is essentially a ninety-minute cinematic joke.

TOOTSIE (1982, COLOR)

Sydney Pollack's *Tootsie* was one of the best produced Hollywood comedies, as well as a hit with critics and aud-

iences. Dustin Hoffman, as out-of-work actor Michael Dorsey, is unable to get a break in his own gender. Dressed in drag, he auditions for the leading matronly role on a soap opera. He/she hits it big on the show, but encounters problems galore in his personal life. Dorsey doesn't tell his girlfriend Sandy, (Teri Garr) what's going on, and she suspects he's either gay or having an affair. At the same time, he's falling in love with the female lead on the show, Julie (Jessica Lange), who's unaware of his true identity. If that's not confusing enough, the male lead on the soap (George Gaynes) is also trying to seduce "Dorothy" (serenading him outside his window in one scene), as is Julie's father (Charles Durning). Pollack, playing George Fields, Dorsey's agent, and Dorsey's roommate Jeff (Bill Murray) are the only ones in on the secret identity. That's where we have to suspend our disbelief—everyone knows a New Yorker can spot a transvestite from a mile away.

The movie's charm comes from Hoffman as Dorothy Michaels. He treats his female alter ego with dignity and takes her seriously. At one point, asking his roommate about a lovely pair of cream palazzos, he even says, "Do these pants make me look hippy?"

THE BEST COMEDIANS TO WORK IN DRAG

Milton Berle

All of the Kids in the Hall

Most of the guys from Monty Python (John Cleese is just too tall to be believable as a woman)

Bugs Bunny

Phyllis Diller

SOME LIKE IT HOT (1959, B&W)

Where *Tootsie* takes pride in treating the premise of female impersonation with dignity, *Some Like It Hot* doesn't.

In Billy Wilder's film, two unemployed musicians played by Tony Curtis and Jack Lemmon, witness the St. Valentine's Day Massacre of 1929 (the Chicago mob battle between Al Capone and rival gangs) and have to clear out of town. Fleeing to Miami in an all-girl band, they pose as . . . well, as girls. They encounter a beautiful singer, Sugar Kane, played by Marilyn Monroe at her most bombshell-like, who Tony Curtis (Joe/Josephine) has the hots for, while Jack Lemmon (Jerry/Daphne) is avidly pursued by a millionaire.

Eventually the mob catches up with Curtis and Lemmon, in a perfect homage to the gangster genre that this film sends up so well. A bit of a nail biter, *Some Like It Hot*'s wonderful script was written by Wilder, with I.A.L. Diamond, and inspired the Broadway musical *Sugar*. The last line of the film is one of the all time greats. After Daphne confesses that she's really a he, her fiancé replies, "Nobody's perfect."

THE PRODUCERS (1967, COLOR)

A cult favorite, Mel Brooks's *The Producers* is the kind of movie that makes people laugh just hearing the premise. A Broadway producer, Max Bialystok (Zero Mostel) on the advice of his accountant, Leo Bloom (Gene Wilder), attempts to get out of his financial hole by making an intentionally bad play. He reasons that when it flops, he won't have to pay his investors. He collects a lot of money from investors (elderly women that he seduces) and sells 25,000 shares. The musical *Springtime for Hitler*, the story of the May love affair between Hitler and Eva Braun and written by a Nazi fanatic, Franz Liebkind (Kenneth Mars), startles everyone by becoming a raging success and wreaking great havoc on Bialystok.

The frequently hilarious cast also includes Dick Shawn and Renee Taylor, and the film features wacky musical numbers that you probably won't see performed in any beauty pageants. It is interesting to watch *The Producers* and note this: Every character is completely nuts.

And if all that isn't enticing enough, Arthur Schleshinger, Jr. called it "An almost flawless triumph of bad taste, unredeemed by wit or style"!

THE TALL GUY (1989, COLOR)

In *The Tall Guy*, Dexter King (Jeff Goldblum) plays the straight guy in a comedy team, the other half of which is sadistic star Ron Anderson (Rowan "Blackadder" Atkinson). Together they perform in a successful stage show called The Rubberface Review. King is frustrated and also highly allergic. Attempting to cure himself of his hay fever he begins a series of shots administered by Nurse Kate Lemmon (Emma Thompson), whom he falls for, and at the same time loses his job. Now an out-of-work actor (we only like to see people *pretending* to be out-of-work actors), King gets the title role in *Elephant!*, a musicalization of *The Elephant Man*. The show is a smash, and King gets a big head and begins an affair with his leading lady. Nurse Lemmon suspects this and dumps him for Anderson. King seeks revenge.

The Tall Guy features the funniest sex scene of any movie ever! And Thompson as his leading lady is the kind of smart, funny woman you wish to see more of in film. You'll also enjoy the staging of *Elephant!*, especially if you're not a big Andrew Lloyd Weber fan. (Let's just say there's a chorus line of tap-dancing elephants and leave it at that.)

AUTHOR! AUTHOR! (1982, COLOR)

If you thought Al Pacino was a great actor in *The Godfather* and *Dog Day Afternoon*, wait till you see him in *Author! Author!*

A successful playwright with a really great apartment, Travalian (Pacino) is about to finish his first play in two years when his wife Gloria (Tuesday Weld) leaves him for another man. She also leaves him with her four children from other marriages, in addition to his own son, Igor (Eric Gurry). Needless to say, his plate is full, but not too full to take up with the star of the production, Alice Detroit (Dyan Cannon). (Radio legends Bob Elliot and Ray Goulding also appear.)

Arthur Hiller directs, and Pacino comes off as father of the year with the kids, who are charming as heck. This is definitely Pacino as you've never seen him. As intense as he was in *The Godfather II*, he is that warm and cuddly in *Author! Author!*

ARSENIC AND OLD LACE (1944, B&W)

A dark comedy classic, Frank Capra's *Arsenic and Old Lace*, is completely devoid of any typical Capra "corn."

Two very dear spinster sisters Martha (Josephine Hull) and Abby Brewster (Jean Adair) lure elderly gentlemen callers to their stately Brooklyn home to terminate their loneliness by poisoning them with elderberry wine. Up shows their nephew Mortimer (Cary Grant) who, horrified, discovers the skeletons in their closets.

The script by Julius J. and Philip G. Epstein, based on Joseph Kesselring's play, is chock full of great lines, like Mortimer's admission: "Insanity doesn't run in my family. It practically gallops!"

Raymond Massey plays the ladies' brother, John Brewster, who believes the victims all perished from yellow fever, and gamely buries them in the basement. John Alexander is the eccentric Uncle Teddy Brewster, who thinks he's Teddy

---

HORROR MOVIES THAT'LL MAKE YOU HOWL

1. *Young Frankenstein*
2. *The Man with Two Brains*
3. *The Little Shop of Horrors*
4. *Night of the Lepus*
5. *An American Werewolf in London*
6. *The Rocky Horror Picture Show*
7. *Tremors*
8. *Dr. Strangelove*
9. *Ghostbusters*
10. *Army of Darkness*

Roosevelt. Peter Lorre and Edward Everett Horton round out the genius cast.

The hysterically timed, uproarious *Arsenic* was filmed in four weeks on one set, a great, spooky, Victorian house near a dilapidated cemetery, for a modest $400,000. It's a hilarious romp that shows what Capra can do when he's not trying to get you to love him and his characters.

LOST IN AMERICA (1985, COLOR)

Albert Brooks's *Lost in America*, which he wrote, directed and acted in, is probably the funniest road movie ever made.

Trading in the genre's traditional Harleys for a nice RV,

Brooks stars as David Howard, a yuppie ad executive who expects to get a promotion, only to be duped and transferred. His wife Linda (Julie Hagerty) has been complaining of boredom. Having no children to tie them down, they forsake their lush life to get wild in this great country of ours.

After purchasing a mobile home, they embark on a tour that gets ravaged in Las Vegas, where Hagerty finds she has a soft spot for gambling.

Lost in America is Brooks at his best, with a typically gemlike Hagerty discovering that destitution has its disadvantages. The comedy addresses the eighties phenomenom of having it all, by chucking it all. Sort of an anti-*Wall Street.*

LOCAL HERO (1983, COLOR)

If you like "Northern Exposure," you'll love *Local Hero.* If you hate "Northern Exposure," you'll still love *Local Hero.* And if you've never heard of "Northern Exposure," where the heck do you live, Jupiter?

A quiet, Scottish picture directed by Bill Forsyth (*Comfort and Joy*), *Local Hero* is the story of Happer (Burt Lancaster), an unbalanced Texas oil baron. Mac (Peter Riegert), an aspiring young exec, is sent to purchase a small Scottish town so Happer's company can drill for North Sea oil. Lancaster, who's so kooky that he hires a psychiatrist (Norman Chancer) to regularly berate him, is also an amateur astronomer. It is this preoccupation that spawns his side mission—to have Riegert "watch the sky for anything interesting."

Don't think that *Local Hero* is an ugly, marauding, American takeover movie. It isn't. It is rather the opposite, as the small Scottish fishing village turns out to be savvy to the ways of a huge American oil company, a comical notion that works perfectly.

Trivia note: Mark Knopfler of Dire Straits did the soundtrack.

KING OF COMEDY (1983, COLOR)

Though it's likely that he won't be remembered as a comedic director, Martin Scorsese's slice-of-life comedic bits are among the most repeated (think about *Goodfellas* and *Mean Streets*). And the two Scorsese picks on this list are every bit as dark as they are comedic.

The King of Comedy stars Robert DeNiro as Rupert Pupkin, a kooky messenger who lives in his parents' basement. His avocation is fantasizing that he is the King of Comedy, and dreaming about his idol, the Johnny Carson-esque Jerry Langford, played by comedic king Jerry Lewis.

After helping Langford escape his annoying fans, Pupkin corners the comedian in his limousine and attempts to try out his self-proclaimed great material. Soon he becomes annoying, hanging out outside Langford's office, where he eventually must be physically removed.

But he doesn't stop there. Oh no.

Sandra Bernhard stars as Masha, the frightening kookette who has a scene with Jerry that should be bronzed. Scorsese's mother, Catherine, provides the voice of Pupkin's off-screen mother, and his daughter, Catherine, plays one of Pupkin's imaginary autograph seekers. To make it a complete family affair, DeNiro's ex-wife Diahnne Abbott also appears. (You might remember her from the scene at the porno movie in *Taxi Driver*.)

AFTER HOURS (1985, COLOR)

To say *After Hours* is set in New York is not quite accurate. The Big Apple is really a character in this most bizarre of all Night-In-The-Life-of-New York movies directed by Scorsese.

As Paul Hackett, Griffin Dunne plays a bored Upper East Side word processor who goes out for an innocent cup of coffee only to meet Marcy (Rosanna Arquette), who spots him reading Henry Miller. A few romantic sparks ignite and Hackett takes her number. Later that evening, he calls her, and she invites him down to Soho. (If New York were a character, the Upper East Side would be played by Ingrid Bergman, Soho by Crispin Glover.) Hackett takes a cab ride, during which all his paper money, a twenty-dollar bill, flies out the window. With that, he is hurled down the proverbial rabbit hole.

Making it to Soho, he finds Marcy's address, but no Arquette. Instead he meets Kiki (Linda Fiorentino), a papier mâché sculptress. Finally Arquette does arrive but is so out of sorts that Hackett leaves, only to discover that his remaining ninety cents is no longer, as of midnight, the subway fare. Now he's trapped in Soho.

Scorsese asks you to suspend your disbelief and take the hand of his Ghost of Bizarre Nights Future through a guided tour of what-ifs. There is murder and mayhem and a curious parade of waifs from Arquette and Fiorentino to Teri Garr as Julie, a hilarious sixties go-go throwback, and Catherine

O'Hara as a rabid Mr. Softee driver. John Heard, Bronson Pinchot and Tommy Chong also appear. As with *The King of Comedy,* you desperately want to laugh during *After Hours* to avoid being scared to pieces.

SMILE (1975, COLOR)

Set in Santa Rosa, California, Michael Ritchie's *Smile* takes a pleasingly black look at beauty pageants.

With a script by TV veteran Jerry Belson, *Smile* plays like a Robert Altman multiple-simultaneous-stories movie. Bruce Dern is "Big Bob" Friedlander, an RV dealer and the beauty contest's main judge. His young son is caught taking undercover shots of the beauties in the buff, with plans to sell them. Upon that discovery, the court orders him to see a psychiatrist before he is allowed to return to school.

Michael Kidd plays Tommy French, a kick-turn type choreographer attempting to advance his fledgling career. Joan Prather, as Miss Antelope Valley, is the sweet-as-peaches-while-doing-anything-to-win character. An almost prepubescent Melanie Griffith has the honor of modeling for some of the nudie pics.

Smile is exceptional, because it's mean and it doesn't care. Later it was reincarnated as a Broadway show, but the movie, though commercially not much more successful, was abundantly superior.

THE SURE THING (1985, COLOR)

Although the two stars (John Cusack and pre-Melrosed Daphne Zuniga) are between the ages of twelve and twenty, you can't call *The Sure Thing* a teen film.

Directed by Rob Reiner before the Meathead thing had really cooled, *The Sure Thing* is a road comedy that begins with two New England college kids, Walter "Gib" Gibson (Cusack), and Alison Bradbury (Zuniga) in their English class (taught by Viveca Lindfors). They are instantly at odds, in a Fred-and-Ginger sort of way. Unfortunately, they find that they have signed up for the same ride to California on Christmas break. Their goals for the journey are as opposite as they are. Cusack is promised a Sure Thing, i.e., sex, (the "Sure Thing" is played by Nicolette Sheridan) and Zuniga is going to meet her very dry betrothed. The drivers of the car are a couple of hilariously nauseating pollyannas (one played by Tim Robbins), but, boy, can they belt out a show tune! On a dare from Cusack, Zuniga frustratedly "exhibits" another side of herself and, after being pulled over, the two are thrown out of the car. They are then forced to hitchhike to California together.

Without being preachy, the film has good messages for the kiddies and is untainted by gratuitous sex. As comedy, it's on the quiet, understated side, but it has its moments—the scenes with Tim Robbins accounting for several of them.

WHERE'S POPPA (1970, COLOR)

Where's Poppa opens with New York lawyer Gordon Hocheiser (George Segal) waking up in the normal fashion—showering, shaving, putting on a suit. Except it's a gorilla suit. In it, he leaps into the room of his mother (Ruth Gordon), at which point she socks him hard, saying "You almost scared me to death." Segal, writhing in pain, responds "Almost isn't good enough."

Carl Reiner directs this cult comedy, the story of a senile Jewish mother and her reluctant mensch son. In a deathbed promise to his father, Segal saddles himself with the care of Gordon, an abrasive woman who downs Pepsi and Lucky Charms for breakfast, which does nothing to help his desperate attempts to escape his single status. Enter lovely Nurse Louise Callan (Trish Van Devere), the only woman Gordon doesn't drive away, as she's a bit odd in her own right. Romance ignites between Segal and Van Devere (who was once married for thirty-two hours), and they soon fall in love, though not without Gordon's hopeless attempts to prevent it.

Don't see this movie on TV, as it is edited with an iron fist. Rent it. (Look for a cameo from the other directing Reiner.) This is the funniest mother/son story since Sophocles's *Oedipus*.

STARTING OVER (1979, COLOR)

An un-macho, un-mustached Burt Reynolds plays Phil Potter, a journalist whose wife Jessica (Candice Bergen) leaves him to develop a singing career, though she's gleefully horrendous. Reynolds moves to Boston, where his brother and sister-in-law, both psychiatrists, get him involved in a very seventies divorced men's support group. They also introduce him to Marilyn Homberg (Jill Clayburgh), a sweet, independent school teacher, who is very seventies single—she eats dinner by herself with wine, candlelight and a feather boa a la *Cosmo*. Phil struggles with his new, scary commitment to Marilyn, as well as the reappearance of Jessica.

Perfectly directed by Alan J. Pakula, Reynolds plays against type and is amazingly vulnerable. *Starting Over* was written by "Mary Tyler Moore Show" alum James L. Brooks (pre-*Terms of Endearment*) from a novel by Dan Wakefield and includes a brief scene with a future "Murphy Brown"-er, Charles Kimbrough.

NIGHT SHIFT (1982, COLOR)

Henry Winkler stars in Ron Howard's *Night Shift* as Chuck Lumley, a sad sack who trades his high-powered accountant's job for the peace and quiet of a night-time morgue shift. Enter the interruption of a lifetime, Bill Blazejowski (Michael Keaton at his zenith) a co-worker who uses the hearse to take a kid (Clint Howard) to the prom for cash.

Keaton calls himself an "idea man." He walks around with a pocket recorder filled with his musings. His latest scheme is to help out Winkler's nice hooker neighbor, Belinda (Shelley Long), who has just lost her pimp, by running a brothel out of the morgue. It's a risky endeavor, and trouble comes from all sides.

With far too many hilarious scenes to recount here, *Night Shift* was written by Babaloo Mandel and Lowell Ganz and produced by Brian Grazer, all of whom later brought you *Splash*. The humor, though, can be summed up in two words: Michael Keaton. Look for a surprising cameo by a future "90210"-er.

THE FRESHMAN (1990, COLOR)

In *The Freshman*, Matthew Broderick plays Clark Kellogg, a kid from Vermont who comes to NYU to study film. (In real life the actor was pushing 30.) He arrives at Grand Central and within five minutes is conned out of his belongings by Victor Ray (Bruno Kirby). He stumbles into Ray a few days later, but sadly, his possessions have already been sold. To make up for it, Ray gets Clark a job with his Uncle Carmine, played by Marlon Brando in a reprisal of his most famous role, not as Jor-El but as Don Corleone, The Godfather. Uncle Carmine, an importer-exporter, gives Clark a job that he says is totally legitimate, although Clark suspects it's mob related. One task includes chauffeuring an exotic animal called a Komodo dragon (which gets lost in a

LITTLE KNOWN EARLY APPEARANCES OF ACTORS IN MOVIES

Kevin Costner as a drunken frat boy in a morgue drawer in *Night Shift*.

Kevin Bacon as a frat brother in *National Lampoon's Animal House*.

Dana Carvey as a parole officer in *Tough Guys* with Burt Lancaster and Kirk Douglas.

Johnny Carson in *Looking for Love* with Connie Francis.

Chris Elliott in *Manhunter*, the precursor to *Silence of the Lambs*.

Sylvester Stallone as a mugger in Woody Allen's *Bananas*.

Bronson Pinchot as Tom Cruise's friend in *Risky Business*.

David Paymer as a cab driver in *The In-Laws*.

Sharon Stone in Allen's *Stardust Memories*.

John Ratzenberger in *The Empire Strikes Back*.

David Letterman in *Cabin Boy*.

---

suburban mall) with the aid of his roommate, Steve Bushak (Frank Whaley).

Penelope Ann Miller stars as Tina, Brando's daughter, and Paul Bentley (from "The Jeffersons") does a great film school prof.

The Freshman doesn't contain any universal truths, there aren't any real epiphanies and the central conflict revolves around a Komodo dragon. But it's gosh darn fun! If for no other reason, though, check it out to see the bulbous Brando on ice skates.

BULL DURHAM (1988, COLOR)

Set in the world of minor league baseball, *Bull Durham* is the story of Crash Davis (Kevin Costner), a power-hitting shortstop on the way out, and Ebby Calvin "Nuke" Laloosh (Tim Robbins) a young, wild pitcher on the way up. Their paths cross as they start their first season with the Class A Durham Bulls. Crash has been brought on board to prepare Nuke for The Show—the major leagues.

Their fates cross again in the form of a woman; Number One fan Annie Savoy (Susan Sarandon). Each season the sexy Savoy chooses one player to tutor in love and literature. This season, however, brings two candidates. Who will she woo? (Trivia bit: It was on this set that Sarandon met Robbins, her future partner and the father of her two children.)

One of the all-time great baseball movies that's not about baseball, *Bull Durham* is thankfully sans a Big Game climax. The quiet, universal theme is one that anyone can relate to. It also has the second funniest sex scene of all time.

Bull Durham was directed by Ron Shelton, who did his residency on the Orioles farm team. Look for the appearance of the famous Clown Prince of Baseball, Max Patkin.

SLAP SHOT (1977, COLOR)

As an aging minor league hockey coach in George Roy Hill's *Slap Shot*, Paul Newman as Reggie Dunlop is drowning in his team's losing streak. News breaks that the team's days are numbered due to the closing of a local steel mill that employs most of the town. Dunlop does a never-say-die, and inspires the team to play the way they have never played

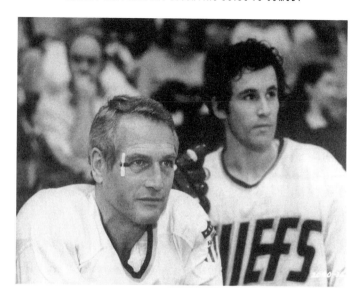

before. Three rookies lead the team to barbarous victories. Suddenly, the crowds start turning out and things are looking sweet. But not in the eyes of leading scorer Ned Braden (Michael Ontkean). He's an Ivy League boy who likes his hockey the old-fashioned way.

In the big game finale, Dunlop's team opposes the toughest club in the league for an unusual ending.

The script comes from Nancy Dowd, whose brother was a hockey player. Not for the squeamish, *Slap Shot* is laden with locker-room language and lots of old-fashioned ugliness.

ADAM'S RIB (1949, B&W)

Spencer Tracy and Katharine Hepburn play husband and wife Adam and Amanda Bonner, two lawyers who happen to be on opposite sides of the same case.

Doris Attinger (Judy Holliday) is being tried for attempting to maim the woman who's having an affair with her husband. Amanda, something of a feminist lawyer, is trying to make the case that the woman's husband would not have been prosecuted had he been in the same position. Adam, a conservative district attorney, is determined to prove her wrong, and the film becomes a battle of the sexes—not only in the case, but in the Tracy-Hepburn relationship as well.

The classic MGM comedy was directed by George Cukor, who also directed Hepburn in the earlier classic *The Philadelphia Story*, and later directed Holliday in the original *Born Yesterday*. The Academy Award-nominated script, written by husband and wife team Garson Kanin and Ruth Gordon, is witty and sharp, but not likely to be shown at any NOW conventions. It is interesting to note that Hollywood is forever trying to duplicate the Tracy-Hepburn chemistry (and still hasn't succeeded). After watching *Adam's Rib*, you will understand why.

USED CARS (1980, COLOR)

In this early Robert Zemekis picture, Kurt Russell plays Rudy Russo, a skeevy but likable head salesman of a used car lot. Across the street is a competing lot owned by Luke Fuchs, the brother of Roy L. Fuchs, the owner of Russell's lot (both Luke and Roy are played by Jack Warden). When Roy dies, Russo and his co-worker conspire to keep it a secret from Luke, and also from Roy's daughter, Barbara.

Another inventive black comedy, *Used Cars* didn't succeed at the box office, due to some equal opportunity offensive humor, but it found new life on video. Television fans will want to look for "Hill Street Blues" 's Betty Thomas as a topless dancer in Rudy's commercial that jams the presidential address. (This feat is by Michael McKean and David L. Lander, "Laverne and Shirley" 's Lenny and Squiggy, respectively.) This is a movie that brings comedy to new heights and bad taste to new depths.

HEARTBURN (1986, COLOR)

In *Heartburn*, Meryl Streep plays Rachel Samstat, a New York writer for a food magazine, who meets Mark Forman (Jack Nicholson), a big-time Washington newspaper columnist, at a wedding. They fall in love and marry, and then the trouble begins.

Heartburn is the story about what a pain in the ass it is to have your marriage fall apart. Mark is a serious playboy who keeps playing the field, and Rachel knows this. She leaves him, forgives him and returns, once. While very pregnant with their second child, though, she discovers an affair he's having with a mutual acquaintance, Thelma Rice (singer Karen Akers).

Jeff Daniels plays Rachel's very supportive editor, and Steven Hill plays the father she runs home to (home is the ritzy Apthorp apartments on Manhattan's Upper West Side), although he's "not very good with these things."

Heartburn takes a universal situation, domestic strife, and applies it to the privileged class. Mike Nichols directs Nora Ephron's screenplay, which is based on her best-selling novel of the same name. Not surprisingly, her real-life husband was Carl Bernstein, one of the *Washington Post* reporters who broke the Watergate scandal. (*Heartburn* was the second movie about this investigative journalist. The first was *All the President's Men*, in which he was played much more flatteringly by Dustin Hoffman. Screwing around on your wife just doesn't rank up there with uncovering presidential misdeeds.)

THE BIG PICTURE (1988, COLOR)

No one in the film biz is safe when Hollywood gets lampooned in Christopher Guest's *The Big Picture.* Kevin Bacon stars as Nick Chapman, an aspiring director who wins the top prize at N.F.I. (a thinly-disguised version of the American Film Institute). A naive Ohio boy, he is suddenly swept up in the world of celebrity. Agents like Neil Glassman (a slightly cross-eyed Martin Short) vie for his attention. In a brilliant restaurant scene, Glassman tells Nick, "I don't want to bullshit you, I don't know you, I don't know your work, but I think you're a very, very talented young man."

Nick gives in to temptation and utterly sells out, leaving behind friends like his cinematographer, Michael McKean. Unfortunately, he finds out that what is hot must go cold, and he learns a bit about the tin hearts of Hollywood people.

Guest's direction takes lots of interesting turns and very funny moments. It's the ultimate movie parody, in the way that *This is Spinal Tap* dealt with "rockumentaries." A cameo-a-go-go, way before Robert Altman's *The Player, The Big Picture* features visits from Roddy McDowall, John Cleese, Eddie Albert and June Lockhart. Jennifer Jason Leigh also stars as a wacky filmmaker who in one scene appears to have an entire rosebush on her head. (Elliot Gould makes an appearance in one of the N.F.I. short films, the director of which is played by his and Barbra Streisand's real-life son, Jason Gould.)

THE IN-LAWS (1979, COLOR)

"Serpentine, Shel, Serpentine!" If you've seen *The In-Laws* you're laughing in recognition at this very moment.

Sheldon Kornpett (Alan Arkin) plays a mild-mannered dentist whose daughter is about to marry the son of Vince Ricardo (Peter Falk). Ricardo may or may not be in the CIA. He says he is, but he seems to be completely nuts. Whatever mess Ricardo is in, Arkin gets dragged along with him. It's a long journey of mayhem as they travel to a South American island, meet a despot and get shot at. Arkin's nebbish is a perfect foil to Falk's nut. *The In-Laws* is the ultimate anti-buddy buddy picture.

Directed by Arthur Hiller, *The In-Laws* is even better than his trio of very successful Neil Simon films, *The Odd Couple*, *The Out of Towners* and *Plaza Suite*. The inspired script was written by Andrew Bergman of *Blazing Saddles* fame.

Open Mikers:
Felicia Michaels

Felicia Michaels didn't grow up wanting to be a standup comic. "I didn't know standup existed," she confesses.

An army brat who grew up in Germany and then moved to a small town in Colorado, Michaels doesn't even recall being particularly funny. "I'd be the one who'd come up with the comeback three days later," she admits, " 'I should've said . . . ' when it wasn't funny anymore."

Her lack of awareness of standup far from inhibited her, "I went to a club," Michaels remembers, "and there was this girl on stage bombing and I thought 'God, I could at least do that.' And I did . . . for quite a while!"

71

Eventually Michaels got an act together and developed her own personal style. And the audience likes it. "They kind of think I'm stupid and shallow," she laughs. Maybe it's because she happens to be a bit of a bombshell and has a seductive, sex-kitten voice. "But I don't care what they think as long as it's about me!" The voice and look are merely vehicles for anything but dumb material, and it's what separates Michaels from the boys.

Michaels, if the truth be known, isn't even really concerned with being a babe. She proudly admits to her thirty-three years. "My rules in comedy are to never lie about my age," she tells, "and to never do period jokes."

The jokes she will do come from various venues. "I was reading in *USA Today*," she says with a set-up quality, "that Bill Clinton has the largest feet of any American president. You know what they say about men with big feet," she pauses, "that they can't get bipartisan support for a health care package."

And the jokes she doesn't get from the paper, she gets from life. "I was born on the day JFK was shot. My brother was born on the day RFK was shot," she reveals. "So Teddy Kennedy wants my mother to have her tubes tied." And speaking of Kennedy, "Did you know Oswald had dyslexia?" she asks. "That was pretty wild that he was in the book depository in the first place. Maybe it was all a mistake. Maybe before dinner his wife simply suggested take-out KFC."

Since a lot of standup involves standing around watching other comedians, it helps to be a fan. Michaels is. She's particularly enthusiastic about fellow comedians, Louis CK, Robert Schimmel, Damon Wayans and Dave Attell. Her biggest inspiration though, is Roseanne. Like her, Michaels desires the sitcom life. Her goals for the immediate future, though, are far less lofty. "I would like to be able to live by my New Year's resolution," she confides, "In January it's like 'I'm going to exercise five days a week, yeah, five days a week.' Then by February it's 'I'm going to ride a bicycle three times a week, yeah, ride that bicycle.' Then by March it's 'I'm going to write a letter on stationery with bicycles on it. Yeah.' "

For now, however, she seems content with her life. "When the show's going good, it's like the audience threw you a surprise party," she reflects. "When it's bad, it's like they want you to leave their party." She remains unthreatened by the rising multitudes who daily attack the open mikes of the world. "There are a lot of comics, but there's always room to make people laugh," she says sweetly. Barely a moment later she adds some advice to aspiring comedians. "Don't do it. There are enough of us already!"

THE RULES OF COMEDY

Everything is funny as long as it is happening to somebody else.

—Will Rogers

In Neil Simon's *The Sunshine Boys*, Willie Clark tells his nephew, probably for the eight-thousandth time, that "words with a *k* are funny. "*Chicken* is funny. *Pickle* is funny. *Kleenex* is funny. *Tomato* is not funny." Willie, an ex-vaudevillian, really believes this is one of the ironclad rules of comedy.

It is.

And it isn't.

That comedy adheres to a set of guidelines and formulas is true. Any comedy expert knows how to time a joke, how to sell it, what kind of rhythm the joke should have. But to acknowledge these rules with any more than a passing nod is to invest them with far too much significance. Of course, if you were to ask a Berle or a Hope or a Lewis, they would tell you that the rules of comedy are as definable and should be regarded as highly as the Periodic Table of Elements.

So we booked an hour or two down in the comedy lab

and compiled a list of both the better-known and more obscure rules of comedy. Here then is an examination and analysis of the rules of comedy. Keep in mind that since the drop/add date has passed, we will not be signing any more forms. As there will be a quiz on this later, we urge you to take copious notes. Good luck.

If it bends it's funny. If it breaks, it's not funny.

In Woody Allen's *Crimes and Misdemeanors*, Lester, an egomaniacal television comic played by Alan Alda, spouts this aphorism relentlessly, like a mantra. As far as we can figure out, what Lester means is that a joke can only be pushed so far before it's not funny. Of course, the determination between when something bends and when it breaks is totally subjective, which leads us to Lester's second rule: Comedy is tragedy plus time. This seems to be an indication that anything sad can become funny give some distance. If this held true, *Macbeth* would be considered a comedy classic by now.

If the audience needs a drop cloth, the performer probably isn't funny.

This rule is not meant to dismiss prop comedy outright; Steve Martin based his very funny early standup on balloon animals and arrows that pierced his head. Even his recent "Great Flydini" bit is about how many things he can pull out of his pants. Comic juggler Michael Davis uses everything from eggs and bowling balls to hatchets in his act. Props can be an integral part of comedy. If the props include food products, paint or tar, however, and if the crowd is in danger of being covered in them, we think the guy probably needs another line of work. Maybe a day job with the sanitation department.

Any comedy movie with a number after its title is not funny.

Notice we didn't say "with a number *in* the title." That's because there are quite a few decent comedies with numbers in their titles, such as *10, 48HRS.* and *The Twelve Chairs.* A number in and of itself does not denote a bad film. It's the placement of the number that does that. Just start approaching territory littered with titles like *Weekend at Bernie's II, Meatballs III,* and *Police Academy 7* (for God's sake), and you realize that this rule is fairly absolute. However, there are exceptions, the most notable being *Rocky V,* and *Airport '75,* two of the best comedies ever made. (You want funny? Catch *Airport '75* and watch as nun Helen Reddy serenades a sick young girl played by Linda Blair, just before Karen Black has to take the controls. This scene is actually funnier than the parody of it in *Airplane.*)

Beware of the standup comic opening his act by asking, "How are you feeling tonight?"

He's simply trolling for cheap applause and his act must automatically be regarded in a lesser light. The same holds true for the comic who, as his ovation dies, tries to rouse the audience by encouraging them to applaud the fabulous work of the emcee: "Come on! Isn't he great? Give it up for him!" The guy's desperation is palapable and the sooner you get him off the stage, the better.

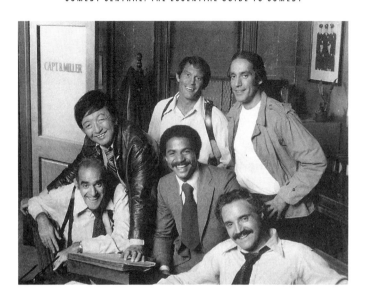

If the name of the club includes the word* Chuckle, Laff *or* Joke, *watch out.
Once and for all, the club itself isn't supposed to be funny. The people on the stage are the funny ones. Generally, the club owners who come up with these names are failed comics themselves, making the club monickers testaments to their mediocrity. So there.

The number of laughs per episode of any sitcom drops in relative proportion to the number of years the series runs.
Simply, the longer the show runs, the less funny it becomes. There are only so many times you can go back to the story well in the course of one series. The characters wear about as well as paper moccasins. Sole exception: "Barney Miller," the only series in television that actually became funnier as

it progressed. The writing and performing improved during every season of the show's eight-year run.

Virtually a one-set show, "Barney Miller" was one of the funniest, yet darkest and most poignant comedies ever shown on television. The writers and producers avoided a problem that plagued most other series—that of having the major characters wear out their welcome. Barney and the other cops in the twelfth precinct could almost be considered supporting players, there to react to the parade of humanity coming through the precinct in every episode.

If the movie worked in French, Spanish or Italian, it's not really a good idea to remake it in English, is it?

Well, is it? Since so much of comedy is based on the culture in which it's produced, and since the subtleties of language are so crucial to verbal humor, something that originally clicked in Europe won't necessarily translate well for English audiences.

Three Men and a Cradle was a French trifle about a trio of Parisian bachelors who find a baby. The question of what these three relatively successful guys were doing living in the same apartment never came up. Who knows? Maybe there are lots of straight guys who live together all over Europe. Remake it in America, change the title to *Three Men and a Baby*, stick Steve Guttenberg, Tom Selleck and Ted Danson in it and that very same element starts raising some unsettling questions, like, "Can't these three movie stars find their own apartments? Why are they living together like frat brothers?"

Dona Flor and Her Two Husbands starred Sonia Braga as a sexy Brazilian woman who lived with her dull fiancé and

---

FUNNIEST CAREER MOVES

McLean Stevenson leaving "M*A*S*H" to make forgettable television shows "Hello Larry," "In The Beginning," "The McLean Stevenson Show" and "Condo."

Shelley Long leaving television to portray the ultimate television character, Carol Brady, in *The Brady Bunch Movie*.

Sonny Bono being elected to Congress.

Ronald Reagan leaving acting.

Sally Struthers giving up acting for fattening food and technical school shilling.

Kathie Lee Gifford leaving dinner theater for television.

---

the ghost of her first husband. When Hollywood got hold of it, the woman became Sally Field, who has long been known as the American Sonia Braga. Jeff Bridges played her husband, a museum curator (gee, what a boring occupation). And her husband's ghost was a tap-dancing James Caan. The producers took a lusty, sexy comedy and turned it into an early-morning cable TV time-filler. The sexual electricity among the three stars couldn't power a reading lamp for a half hour. And they wondered why it didn't do better business.

The rule of threes

Very simply, this rule states that things are funniest in threes. Ever hear of The Two Stooges? What about Four Blind Mice? And though there were five Marx Brothers, only three of them were funny. Think about the last time you heard a joke involving a priest and a rabbi. There's always a minister along for balance, isn't there? Why? Its a question of timing. Read the joke below:

A guy dies and goes to hell. He swears there's been a mistake and goes right to the head guy.

"Devil, there's been a mistake," the guy says. "I don't belong here."

The devil says, "No, I checked your credentials and you are definitely in the right place."

The guy says, "I'm so surprised, I don't know what to do now that I'm here."

The devil tells him, "Don't worry, you'll find your peer group. Come, I'll show you around."

They come upon a group of noisy people. "Who are those people?" the guy asks.

"Those are Catholics," the devil says.

The guy asks, "Why are they here?"

The devil says "Oh, they ate meat on Friday."

The pair moves on to another room full of noisy folks. "Who are they?" the guy asks.

"Those are Jews," says the devil.

The guy asks "Why are they here?"

"They didn't go to synagogue."

Finally, the devil and the guy arrive at a room full of people, this one much quieter than the first two.

The guy asks, "Who are these people?"

"They're Episcopalians," says the devil.

"Why are they here?"

"They ate shrimp with their salad forks."

Jewish, Catholic, punch line. Add Hindus and Baptists and you're in trouble.

The rule of threes is one of those rules, like most in this chapter, that's better if it's simply observed, rather than articulated. Once you start saying these things out loud, you run the danger of becoming an insufferable bore. So remember, don't state the rules. Just know them.

OPEN MIKERS:
JIM BREUER

To watch Jim Breuer onstage is to know that you're looking at the funniest guy in class. Whether he's playing a streetwise New York pigeon or a drunken stomach expelling all its contents to "get out the same way you came in," Jim's "I dare you not to laugh" style has attracted attention in clubs across the country. But his early gigs weren't in comedy clubs. The self-proclaimed "frustrated rocker" began working in rock clubs around Long Island opening for local bands, where he did material that he characterizes as "dumb high school stuff."

A move to Florida made Jim start taking standup seriously. "I did a lot of open mike stuff and a lot of amateur stuff. My dad was in the Elks Club and

I'd work a talent show there." After about three months, Jim landed an emcee spot at a local club, which gave him stage time to work on his stuff, if not the ability to pay his bills. "Half the time, I didn't get paid. The other half, it might be a hundred bucks a week. But to me, that was a lot."

With recommendations from the manager of the club, Jim was able to work other clubs on the road, where the work was frequent, but the paydays weren't necessarily. "To drive from Mobile, Alabama, to Texas and then have the guy say 'I can't pay you, but I can give you your room for free' is a real drag. And that happened many, many times."

And, Jim says, working as an emcee is murder on a comic's material, since the emcee is essentially working for the club, making announcements, directing traffic between the other acts and, incidentally, doing some of his own material. "The club owner tells the emcee, 'Listen, I need all these announcements done, then do two minutes of your stuff and then bring up the next act.' And it's frustrating because you want to try this stuff out and you're up there and you have to say 'Friday is free chicken night and on Saturday, bald people get in for free. Two Jews walk into a bar . . . please welcome your next comedian . . . ' "

Eventually, the logistics of the business began dictating that Jim get paid every time he worked. "On the road, there are usually three comics: an emcee, a middle and a headliner. When you start performing as a middle, people start to take you a little more seriously."

It was the cutthroat attitude of other comics that gave Jim the idea that he was getting better onstage. "When I started performing as a middle, certain headliners would come up to me and say 'Look, why don't you do a little less time tonight.' And I'd realize that the guy was having a tough time following me. And club owners were starting to tell me that they wanted me to work as a headliner."

As his standup act began to be seen by more people, Jim got a part in a late-night TV sketch comedy series called "Uptown Comedy Club." "That helped me because I was able to tell people in the industry that I was on TV. And I learned about working in front of a camera. Very important."

Despite the grueling schedule of the show, Jim felt it was important to maintain his standup work. "I felt like I had to be in a club every single night." Through it all, though, his writing process remained the same. "I'm not someone that sits down and writes. I did write sketches while I was doing 'Uptown,' but my own stuff basically came out of what I was living. It could be a problem at home or just something that pissed me off. I could show you my notebooks, which are basically just ideas; stuff like 'me and my wife arguing about shoes.' It's very hard for me to make things up. So the stuff that really works for me is everything that I've observed."

If it sounds like a risky way to go onstage, Jim thinks otherwise. "I thought of it that way, but then I watched other comics who were just winging it. And I thought 'where does he get the balls to just go up there that confident?' Now, when I get up there, I have that confidence. When you're up there with only a general idea and it starts working, you start thinking 'How far can this go?' It's just great when it works."

Now, Breuer has gone where only a select few performers

before him have gone—to the cast of "Saturday Night Live."

Although TV is a big part of Jim Breuer's master plan, a nightclub stage is where he really feels at home. "You know, I've been to a lot of concerts, and the ones that I really love are when I know the band is really into it. That's why, when I'm up there, and they know I'm having a good time, the crowd is having a good time."

They're Called "Records." They Were Very Popular Until About . . .

Comedy is the blues for people who can't sing.
                                                    —Chris Rock

"When I was your age," you hear yourself tell the gang of youths glued to "An Evening at The Improv," "we couldn't just turn on the TV twenty-four hours a day and get standup." Your voice rises, "WE had to LISTEN to comedy ALBUMS!"

They look at you the way you once looked at your Uncle Bernie, who couldn't stop yammering on about the magic of radio and his Little Orphan Annie secret decoder ring.

"You kids have it so easy," you say, wiping the rabid drool from your chin, "You make me sick. NOW GET OUT OF MY SIGHT!"

Comedy albums. Even the name sounds archaic—like something that should be heard on a crank victrola. But there really was a time, when men were men and the dark side ruled the galaxy and, especially if you were underage, you could only hear Richard Pryor or Flip Wilson if you had a turntable.

It seems peculiar now, in an age where—forget prime time and movies—you can't even watch a commercial for a corn chip, breath mint or credit card without seeing the face of your favorite headliner. But comedy albums, way back when, pretty much had the job of servicing all your standup needs. Most people couldn't get to Town Hall to see Lenny Bruce live, and those that did made it only once a year. So, they'd buy his album.

A lot of eggs went into the vinyl basket for a comic. It ate up his entire act for a whole year. Analogous to the one-hour TV specials, or concert videos of today, records were committed to the memory of any kid who wanted to be cool. (You'd better know Carlin's seven words you aren't allowed to say on television, or stay away from my locker!) But unlike videos, or standup concert films, you didn't have the movements to go along with the words. When you listen to some of these albums, you miss something the live audience gets: the faces, expressions and gestures of the comedian. The wonderful moment when a standup comic reels you back after taking a sip of water.

As radio did before television, standup albums force you to use the theater of the mind—or imagination as we grown-ups like to call it. It feels kind of virtuous to be entertained without turning on the cable box, sort of brings you closer to Walton's Mountain. (We suggest listening to them sipping an egg cream, maybe wearing a raccoon coat or varsity sweater.)

The list that follows comes from the heyday of comedy albums, the 1960s and 1970s. That's not because nothing funny came out in the eighties and nineties, but because albums were supplanted by the aforementioned one-man concerts on cable and video. In fact, some very funny material has been released recently on vinyl and CD; Adam Sandler, Steven Wright, Eddie Murphy, Sam Kinison and Andrew Dice Clay all produced successful albums. But still there's no comparison.

To prove this point, we ask you to guess who the dominant winner in the Grammy category of Best Comedy Album over the last several years has been. Give up? P.D.Q. Bach by Peter Schickele. He does sendups of classical music pieces. Defense rests.

The selections we chose are not simply the funniest, but they are the standards that all other comedy albums can be measured by. They typify their creators' style and prove to be the inspiration of much of what is deemed funny today. You will hear, bits by, say, Cosby that were taken a step further by, say, Eddie Murphy. You may even think Murphy does it better than Cosby, or that Martin Lawrence does it better than Eddie, for that matter. But that's sort of like saying the Flintstones' car was too hard on the feet. Sure, but where would we be today without it?

LENNY BRUCE

There is a bit on "Lenny Bruce—American" called "How To Relax Your Colored Friends at Parties." If you're unfamiliar with Bruce, you may have just flinched. Now imagine if this were 1960, when the album was originally recorded. You probably would have passed out. Bruce plays a white guy speaking to a black man (played by his guitarist, Eric Miller) at a party. Bruce begins by proposing a toast to black

---

THE CLOSEST THING TO ACTUALLY SEEING LENNY BRUCE

Lenny (1974). Dustin Hoffman's portrayal of the self-destructive, inventive comic.

Lenny Bruce (1967). An unedited film of a San Francisco nightclub performance in August 1965.

Lenny Bruce Without Tears (1975). A documentary that includes clips and segments of Bruce's acts, as well as interviews with Bruce and comedians influenced by his work.

---

fighter Joe Louis, then to Bojangles—"All you people can tap dance, right, got that natural rhythm born right in you." Getting progressively loaded, Bruce's character offers the black man food—watermelon and fried chicken. "I'd like to have you over to the house," he finishes, "but I have a sister . . ." Whoa! Can you imagine? It took people a while to get the point that even the most enlightened white liberals have no idea how to interact socially with African Americans. And only then did you get the humor.

There aren't too many people unaware of Lenny Bruce's role as trailblazer. Aside from taking on race, he tackled sexual mores, the Pope and religion, obscenity and censorship laws. He even went after the progressive, finger-poppin' beatniks of the 1950s who comprised his audience.

The material on "American" and "Togetherness" is surprisingly up to date. "The Phone Company" on "Togetherness," is about how Bruce never looks up a telephone number, and instead automatically dials 411. But he's so nervous, he forgets the number the operator gives him. He dials 411 again, but this time disguises his voice in case, out of the ten billion operators, he gets the same one and she remembers him! He doesn't want to be noticed because The Phone Company is a monopoly—if you get in bad with them you're back to paper cups joined by a string.

Okay, the phone company is no longer a monopoly, but in thirty-five years that's about all that's changed. (An example of what hasn't changed: Howard Stern, like Bruce, is still absurdly fined by the FCC for obscenity.) And there's Bruce's way of speaking; he's a true hipster given to the random "Dig this" and "Solid!" There are also some allusions you may not understand, but have no fear. The re-releases contain glossaries of terms and references to clue you in. For example, "Knish: Jewish delicacy of ground meat, spinach, and spices wrapped in savory dough" or, "Shelly Berman: Jewish comic during the Golden Age of cabaret comedy, given to uncontrolled tantrums on and off stage." Dig it!

GEORGE CARLIN

Big fans of George Carlin may not think the 1972 album, "Class Clown," is his finest. It is, however, the best demonstration of how Carlin used his life—growing up Irish Catholic in New York City—to create his act. His reflections, including those about priests and confessions, encompassed his entire life experience in a way that hadn't been done before.

Indulging the fourth-grader in us all, Carlin demonstrates some of the finer points of class clownitude: Hawaiian Nose

Humming, Playing the Head and the various noises one can make with the mouth and armpit, with special mention given to crowd-pleasing flatulence. "There were a lot of ways to make the fart sound when you were a kid," Carlin considers. "It was an important sound, I guess. We found so many ways to make it."

On the inside jacket of the album, which was recorded live at the Santa Monica Civic Auditorium, an acknowledgment reads, "Special thanks to Leonard Schneider for taking all the chances." Leonard Schneider is Lenny Bruce, and his influence on Carlin is profound.

The record's most famous bit is a hearty nod, almost an homage, to Lenny Bruce. "Seven Words You Can Never Say on Television" is Carlin's gentle jab at obscenity and censorship. "Be careful," he cautions about the Nasty Seven. "They can infect your mind, curve your spine and lose the war for the allies." He goes on to recite the list, rapid wildfire: Shit, Piss, Fuck, Cunt, Cocksucker, Motherfucker and Tits. (Wooooo-weeee! That feels good!) Taking apart the list, word by word, Carlin illustrates the absurdity. "Tits doesn't even belong on this list!" he argues. "It's such a friendly sounding word. It sounds like a snack food, New Nabisco Tits!"

The cover photo has Carlin donning long hair and beard, and wearing a fully open denim shirt. He is surrounded by smiley faces, hearts and peace signs. The sensibility and language of the early seventies permeates the recording, promising a "Man!" for every one of Lenny Bruce's "dig its".

BILL COSBY

When you get to the end of "Niagara Falls" on Bill Cosby's "Wonderfulness," you find yourself waiting expectantly. You hear no more sound. You get up and look at the record player, and you see that it is at the end. No more. Over. You're sad. You see, the title of the album is also its description.

Cosby is at the start of his career here, doing material about the beginning of his life. It is less standup than storytelling, with punch lines woven throughout. Based on very personal experience, "Wonderfulness" is definitely from the guy who would later bring you the best-selling book, *Fatherhood* (and maybe, someday, *Grandfatherhood*?)

Remember Fat Albert and The Cosby Kids? Cosby had a great memory for the trials of kidhood and was brilliant at dramatizing them. "Wonderfulness" is no exception. In "Chicken Heart," Cosby adeptly describes how his parents didn't believe in babysitters. They wouldn't leave him with a stranger—instead, they left him alone. The only way to keep him from getting out of bed when they were gone was to scare him with a lie. "Now to make sure you don't get out of this bed," his mother would tell him, "we've placed over a hundred black, poisonous snakes around your bed. And if you so much as place a toe out there, they're going to bite you, you're going to swell up and be dead until

99

morning." Cosby whines that he doesn't see them and, his mother tells him it's because they're invisible. Then, they leave. "Boy I'm so sick of this place I'm going to run away from home," Cosby cries. "Always putting black snakes." He addresses the serpents, half angry, more scared, yelling, *"Snakes? You get out of here! This is not your room this is my room, now you get out of here! I don't care who sent you here, this is my room. I didn't ask you to come in here, nasty snakes! Snakes do you hear me talking to you, huh? Snakes. I gotta go to the bathroom. C'mon have a heart on a guy will ya? Are you out there? Listen, snakes, now don't you bite me, I'm going to put my toe out there. Don't bite it, just give it a little snakey lick (lik-a-lik-a-lik-a-lik) C'mon, okay you listen, you can bite it just a little, but don't put none of your juice in it . . ."* It's a riot, but you have to hear Cosby do it to truly appreciate just what "wonderfulness" is.

ALBERT BROOKS

You didn't know Albert Brooks began as a standup comic? Boy, are you in for a treat! This selection, "Albert Brooks: Comedy Minus One" was recorded in 1973.

An extraordinarily innovative production, "Comedy Minus One" is one and a half sides of standup featuring such bits as "Another Kooky Krazy Kall." Long before the Jerky Boys, Brooks was pulling pranks. Here he disguises his voice and calls a pet store, wanting to buy ten parakeets. A woman answers and he asks her how many parakeets she has in stock,

"Seven or eight," she replies.

"I'm going to need ten," says Brooks in his "funny voice."

"Well," the woman responds, "we have another store in the area. We could get them from there."

"Oh, you have to go to another store?" Brooks asks, snickering.

"Yes," the woman tells him.

"Well," concludes Brooks, "I'll have to think about it, and I'll get back to you later." And that's it. Are you thinking it's not very kooky and krazy? Or even funny? Herein lies the brilliance: the fact is that only Albert Brooks can deliver this material and actually get laughs.

The last quarter of the album is an old vaudeville routine about taking a car into the mechanic. But the mechanic's punch lines are left out—they are to be performed by the album purchaser, using the script supplied. It is great fun, and if you get really good you can record your own album!

STEVE MARTIN

Recorded at The Boarding House, a small club in San Francisco, "Let's Get Small" is vintage Steve Martin before he became bigger than The Beatles at the Hollywood Bowl. They coined the phrase "Rock and Roll Comic" to describe Martin phenomena—ironically, the very thing that made him quit standup.

Martin's humor was something of a reaction to the tone of standup that preceded him. He was fresh and silly. There wasn't a lot of angst and darkness. He even wore a white suit (which eventually matched his hair). Here is a comic

who's not into his hipness, and who doesn't cloud his bits with esoteric, pretentious references. You've got the arrow through the head, the peppy banjo playing, and balloons folded into animals. But make no mistake, you do have to be smart to "get" him.

A totally unalienating performer, Martin even shares some hints on how you, too, can be funny. "People come to me and they say 'Steve . . . Martin, is there some way I could be funny, too?' Well, here's a couple of jokes I like to pass on to the crowd, and these are jokes you can play on your friends, if you enjoy the good practical joke. Next time you go out with your friends, before you go, you secretly put an atom bomb in your nose, then when you get there you pretend like you're going to sneeze, you give it the old 'Ahhh, Ahhhh . . . !' Then you set off the bomb [bomb noise]. It's funny."

One of Martin's signature phrases comes from this album. "Well, excuuuuuse me!" was later heard on television commercials, seen on T-shirts and bumper stickers . . . even your Social Studies teacher and grandmother knew it. To think, it all started with a bit that went something like this.

Martin asks for "some mood lighting, a blue spot or something." He gets nothing. He plays it cool. "I'm kind of pissed off about this, I've been going on all week. . . . You'd think by now they'd have it under control." His anger slowly builds, until Martin is complaining about the hippies running the club who are more interested in taking drugs than doing "a good show for the people." Now he's starting to get mad. "It's just a matter that I'm out here on stage, and it's my ass out here, and I'm giving and I'm giving and I'm giving and I keep giving and I give some more and I make a simple request, I say 'Hey, could I possibly have a blue spot?' But I guess the lighting crew feels they know a little more," really yelling now, "ABOUT SHOW BUSINESS THAN I DO, ALTHOUGH I'VE BEEN IN THE BUSINESS A FEW YEARS AND I THINK I KNOW WHAT WORKS BEST, I'M SORRY, BUT I'M ANGRY, I COME OUT HERE AND I CAN'T GET A LITTLE COOPERATION FROM THE BACKSTAGE CREEEEWWWW? EXCUUUUUUUUSSSSE MEEEEEE!" Martin has perfect command of the art of taking something as far as it can go, and then taking it further, and then further still.

ROBERT KLEIN

No one is more sick of the phrase "observational humor" than we are, but it's impossible to describe Robert Klein without using it. We'll try our best to economize.

The cuts on Robert Klein's 1974 album, "Mind Over Matter," read like an observational humor catalogue; "100% Undetectable Hairpiece," "Juergen's Myasthenia," "Wallowing in Watergate," "Obligatory Drug Bit: First Time Stoned." Klein, if not invented, then molded this genre of standup into what it is today. You may be happy

about that or not—it depends on whether you're a fan of observational humor (last time, promise).

Klein, the precursor to Jerry Seinfeld, Dennis Miller and Steven Wright, among others, fills "Mind Over Matter" with topical material that holds up twenty years later, (Okay, so Watergate is not the buzzword on everyone's lips today.) Substitute the moniker "New Age" for the cut entitled "Mysticism," and you're fully up to date.

"I've had too many people guess my sign," Klein begins. "They take twelve guesses." He continues with this familiar yarn. "Have you ever seen a horoscope column in the paper that would not work with your day? Well, you stretch it a little. 'A good day to ask for a raise.'" He mocks, "Yeah! Right on! If I had a job, it would be a good day to ask for a raise."

"No News News (Milton Lewis)" is a bit about the slow news days when local reporters—in this case Milton Lewis— go into the field to fill up air time.

"If you're looking for something to do in Fun City," Klein announces in grating, street-reporter voice, "there's no better place to look than East 33rd Street where Mr & Mrs. J. Capito have been stringing pearls for fourteen years. Mr. & Mrs. Capito, how long have you been stringing pearls?"

Klein, as Capito, in a dull voice answers "fourteen years."

Klein/Lewis then wonders "What color pearls do you use?"

Klein/Capito responds, "Red, Milton. Green. We used blue last week didn't we?"

Klein/Lewis questions, "Do you like stringing the pearls?"

Klein/Capito returns, "Yes we all enjoy it very much."

"Mind Over Matter" is the name of the final number, a song actually, written and sung by Klein. (And in case you were worried, there's enough shots of Klein with bad seventies hair to please even the most discerning palate.)

WOODY ALLEN

Woody Allen was not a great movie director—in fact, he was not even a director at all— when introduced to audiences on the album "Stand Up Comic."

Comprised of actual routines done in nightclubs, the three sections of the record come from 1964 (at Mr. Kelly's in Chicago), 1965 (The Shadows in Washington D.C.) and 1968 (a Eugene McCarthy fundraiser in San Francisco). The material is quintessential 1960s New York Jewish intellectual. Surprise!

In *Annie Hall*, which you remember because you've seen it five thousand times, Allen plays Alvy Singer, a

105

standup comic. There are even two scenes (on the Dick Cavett show and at the University of Wisconsin with Allison Porchnik/Carol Kane) in which he does his act. "Stand Up Comic" includes some of the same jokes.

In addition to familiar material, you will also recognize the future director's gift for storytelling. His early material comes across much like his early movies and, of course, is loaded with great laughs.

"I got married by a reformed Rabbi in Long Island, a very reformed Rabbi. A Nazi."

"I was thrown out of NYU for cheating on my metaphysics final. I looked within the soul of the boy sitting next to me."

"I was hired by a very dyed-in-the-wool ad agency on Madison Avenue to sit in an office and look Jewish . . . I'd read my memos right to left."

There is an odd resonance to some of the bits. Maybe you can see what we mean:

"I don't know if you read in the paper but my ex-wife is suing me. I made a nasty remark about her. She lives on the Upper West Side of Manhattan, and she was coming home late one night, and she was violated. That's how they put it in the New York paper. They asked me to comment, and I said knowing my ex-wife it was not a moving violation."

NATIONAL LAMPOON

You loved their magazine. You loved their movies. Now love "National Lampoon's Gold Turkey: Radio Hour/Greatest

Hits." Probably the last well-produced radio show, "Gold Turkey" is the best of that treasure trove.

Let's first see if you recognize any of the people involved with "National Lampoon's Radio Hour." Ever hear of John Belushi? Bill Murray? Gilda Radner? How about Brian Doyle-Murray and Harold Ramis? Christopher Guest, maybe Chevy Chase?

You're probably chomping at the bit right about now, and you should be. This album has more gems than a Ft. Lauderdale canasta table. The rich material comes in the form of spoofs, comedy bits and songs.

"Well-Intentioned Blues," sung and co-written by Christopher Guest, does for white blues what "Spinal Tap" did for heavy metal. "I wish I was a negro, with lots of negro soul, so I could stay true to my ethnic roots and still play rock and roll. If I was a funky negro, eatin' soul food barbecue, I wouldn't have to sing the middle class, liberal, well-intentioned blues." The verses go on to include Indians, ("a grown-up Sioux papoose,") Mexicans, ("Wetbacks on a strike in a lettuce patch") and "a slant-eyed peasant farmer with Viet Cong stashed underneath my thatch." This was before political correctness was invented!

Stan Sawyer and Brian McConnachie in their "Public Disservice" message advise you to "Never send care packages to the 'so-called' starving families in Europe, because they're not starving at all! Can you afford to live in Europe? No. You can't even afford to visit Europe." You know Jack Handy's "Deep Thoughts" on "Saturday Night Live." Uh huh. 'Nough said.

A "Masterpiece Theatre"-type production of Fyodor Dostoyevsky's *The Idiot* is sublimely sent up in "Front Row

Center." After a refined, British-accented Christopher Guest recites the very proper introduction, replete with over-pronounced Russian names (including Alexander Solzhenitsyn because, why not!) Enter Bill Murray as The Idiot. In a very zany voice, slightly off mike, he screams, "Everybody get out of here. There's a lobster loose! Oh Holy God! Everybody get out of here, he's vengeful! Quick cover yourself in hot butter and carry lemons just in case."

And for the bad seventies hair buffs, there's a back-cover bonanza of no less than—count 'em—twenty-eight righteous dos!

MONTY PYTHON

Good friends should never discuss politics, religion, and British humor. Wars have begun over Benny Hill. (The pro-Bennys never had a chance in those tea length, chiffon fatigues.)

Frankly, a lot of Americans hate, or at least claim to hate, English humor. Unfortunately, that sort of blanket bias causes the dismissal of some superb British material that would stand up in any language!

Monty Python is one of the targets of Transatlantic Humor Prejudice. A hugely successful release in 1995 of their much touted CD-ROM "Complete Waste of Time," though, proved that the naysayers are outnumbered. The user-friendly troupe that included folks who went on to become John Cleese, Terry Gilliam, Graham Chapman, Michael Palin, Eric Idle and Terry Jones, continues to escort virgin fans into new decades. (Incidentally, the CD-ROM

includes really cool screen savers and something that can make the keys of your computer sound like a typewriter.)

"Matching Tie and Handkerchief," Monty Python's 1973 album, is unlike most of this list, because it's not a recording of an act or a compilation of night club appearances. It is three sides of well-produced bits, something like old radio. Yes, you read right. *Three* sides. One of the gimmicks of this album was that you could pick up the needle at the end of side two, put it down on the inner grooves, and get more comedy. Another gimmick was a removable paper tie and handkerchief on the album cover. (Which has been replaced by a big, empty, white spot on the cassette. Oooh fun!)

The material shows its Britishosity in a few highbrow references (Oscar Wilde, The Prince of Wales) and by being a little more clever than you're used to. "Wide World of Novel Writing" is a take-off on "Wide World of Sports," with a play-by-play of Thomas Hardy writing a novel. "And here comes Hardy walking to his desk," the announcer brays, "He dips the pen in the ink and he's off, it's the first word, but it's not a word, it's a doodle!" There is a goof on Australians simply titled "Bruces" and "The Cheese Shop," about a visit to a cheese shop without any cheese.

Probably the most imaginative bit, though, is "Talking in the Terrier." A man walks into a pet shop and it goes something like this:

MAN: Good morning, I'd like to buy a cat.

STOREKEEPER: I've got a lovely terrier.

MAN: No, no, I want a cat really.

STOREKEEPER: Uh, how about this then?

MAN: Well, that's a terrier.

STOREKEEPER: Look, I'll tell you what, I'll file his legs down a bit, take his snout out, stick a few wires in his cheek. Make a lovely cat, that would!

MAN: No, no, no, it's still not a proper cat. . . . It wouldn't meow.

STOREKEEPER: No but it would howl a bit.

And so will you!

BOB NEWHART

One bleak night a week in comedy clubs across the country, there will be an open mike showcase. It might be called

Funniest Bank Tellers or Funniest Dog Groomers, and these
average Joes will get up and do
their shtick with their drunken
friends out there cracking up.
Some of these fair-weather
comics actually think they are
really good, and they go into
their boss's office the next day
and quit. They then join the
ranks of the quadrillion comedians working today. People
think because there are a quad-

rillion comedians that everyone can be one. Or they know
this guy in their office who's so freakin' funny he could be
on Jay Leno. This Is a Nineties Phenomenon.

Yes! There was a time when a barber was happy cutting
hair, and a lawyer was happy chasing ambulances. And that's
what made Bob Newhart unique in the sixties. He was a
mild-mannered, Catholic accountant from Chicago who
bucked the system and made good.

Enough about that, let's talk about "The Button Down
Mind Strikes Back!" the successful followup to "The Button
Down Mind of Bob Newhart."

Until this album, Newhart's trademarks were his phone
calls. He would be on one end of the phone, reacting to the
imaginary other speaker. On "The Button Down Mind
Strikes Back!" Newhart gets a little more sketch/story/bit
oriented.

A sort of pre-Garrison Keillor, Bob Newhart does the
cleanest material you ever will hear. You can definitely buy

111

this album for your in-laws. There are jokes about the age of technology, retirement parties and the revolutionary war.

At times it's a bit dated. Newhart does what all comedians make fun of now. He gives you the imaginary situation as a setup, then says "It might have gone something like this . . ." and goes into the bit. But he's also ahead of his time, making fun of the comic transition. "My problem is that I want to start talking about airplanes now and there is no logical way to get out of what I was talking about, and talking about airplanes . . . So I will try this. In the war movies, they will always have one shot of the dog fights with the airplanes . . . speaking of airplanes . . ." And he goes into a bit about a low-cost, no-frills airline, "The Grace L. Ferguson Airline (And Storm Door Co.)" in which the inept pilot comes out and asks the passengers "Have any of you ever been to Hawaii? This gentleman here? It's kind of liver-shaped isn't it sir? Sir, as we're coming in would you mind coming into the cabin and pointing it out?" And if you can imagine it with Newhart's deadpan delivery, you're probably halfway to the record store now.

Open Mikers:
Todd Barry

Todd Barry looks like Barry "Greg Brady" Williams. The difference is Barry Williams never performed a standup act on Conan O'Brien, while, you guessed it, Todd Barry has.

Though he was born in New York, Barry grew up in Florida. It was there, in North Miami where he did his first open mike night. "I had gone to this comedy club once or twice, and I watched the other comics do it," he recalls, "and I had this sick feeling that I should at least try."

Seven years later he's still at it, though comedy wasn't Barry's lifelong dream. "I never wanted to be a comic, though I guess I was always funny," tells the 30-year-old comic. "I was in bands when I was in college. I guess I sort of wanted to do that, but it was too hard. Comedy is the only thing I'm confident that I'm fairly decent at."

The confidence is what allows him to handle the obstacles: specifically, hecklers. "I start a joke, 'I have roaches' and some guy yells 'I got roaches!' Like who the hell cares?" (The joke continues. "So I laid out Combat roach traps, and I had this woman over not too long ago—about two years ago—and she says 'Todd, you don't have a roach problem do you? These aren't roach traps are they?' And I say 'Roaches? These are speakers baby, haven't you ever heard of floor tweeters?' ")

"The act is sarcastic," he starts to consider. "I guess people could think I'm an asshole, that I'm not as nice as I am." He doesn't apologize. He shouldn't. It's what makes him a standout performer. He doesn't wear funny glasses, or a kooky bow tie or hammer watermelons. He is armed only with attitude and jokes that are a cut or two above the rest.

Though Barry didn't want to be a comic, he does remember liking Bill Hicks and Andy Kaufman on the early Lettermans. If there had been comedy courses back then, would he have taken one? "No. And I hope that the people that take them today don't think it's like learning to be a typist," he advises, "I think the people that teach them have suspect qualifications. They aren't even comics."

With or without the classes, standups are sprouting up relentlessly. However, the scene has changed since the late eighties and there aren't as many clubs as there once were. Barry feels that their disappearance won't necessarily allow a survival of the fittest. "Not only the strong survive; there are really bad people who do really well." He hastens to add, "I'm sure if two hundred quit, the world wouldn't suffer."

His final words for those who undertake the path of standup are not to be taken lightly. "Be funny," he warns, "and don't annoy people."

KNOW WHAT I SAW LAST NIGHT? OR THE BEST EPISODES OF THE BEST SITUATION COMEDIES EVER

There is nothing in which people more betray their character than in what they laugh at.
                    —Johann Wolfgang von Goethe

Thus far, we have filled this book with weighty musings on universal human truths, poignant ideologies and keys to man's eternal struggle to use the Aynsworth Socioanthropological record.

At this juncture, though, we turn to situation comedies, and, well, don't be mad, but the most in-depth insight we have about them is that we think they're a real scream.

This does not preclude lofty pontification. There is a lot to be said about sitcoms. For example, a bit of history. Did you know that Aristophanes wrote the first sitcom? It was called *Hot l Acropolis* and it starred a young Abe Vigoda as the saucy bellhop Herpes. Funny, but totally derivative of Neil Simon.

There really *is* a history to sitcoms; however, it will be limited to our favorites, the Firsts, the ones who started it all, the ones that made every other network on the block say, "I want a show just like that one!" And they got them!

But we don't care about the wannabes. We care about the bes.

Think about "The Dick Van Dyke Show" (1961–66), the earliest sitcom about a TV writer's work and home life. This tried-and-true formula first appeared here, and it still works today. Where? Think "Murphy Brown," "The Mary Tyler Moore Show," "NewsRadio," "The Larry Sanders Show." What made it succeed, however, was not only the setup, but the great writing of Carl Reiner, Jerry Paris and Sheldon Leonard. A real precedent setter.

Or go back even further, to 1951 when a certain red-haired comedienne and her Cuban, bongo-playing husband teamed up for one of the most successful runs in sitcom history. The popularity of "I Love Lucy" was due in part to the odd pairing of the real life couple that made the show believable, the superlative writing that highlighted Lucy's universal aim to be famous and the brilliant physical comedy talents of its leading lady. It didn't matter what Lucy was up against—in her wacky way, she triumphed. "I Love Lucy" was one of the first sitcoms to mirror real life. For example when Lucille Ball gave birth to Desi Arnaz, Jr., forty-four million people tuned in for the reenactment on the subsequent show.

Move over to the left, or should we say step behind the white line to "The Honeymooners" (1955–56). Not an incredibly successful show at its inception (only thirty-nine episodes were taped), its popularity grew until the "lost episodes" now nestle comfortably beside Ms. Ball in Syndication Heaven, where these shows make the Energizer bunny look like a geriatric patient on life support. Ralph and Alice Kramden and Ed and Trixie Norton were no strangers to physical comedy, either, and they did it all in one dingy room, sans glamour. They brought blue-collar comedy out of the closet and into the kitchen. Remember, they didn't even have a living room; in fact, on only one episode did they have a TV—a little something to give every viewer the chance to feel superior to them. Their true-to-life approach resonates in newer shows such as "Roseanne," "Grace Under Fire" and "Townies."

"All in the Family" (1971–83) was another ground-breaker that brought a new kind of family into the American home, with its controversial patriarch, Archie Bunker, and the first show to poke fun at political correctness. A testament to the importance of "All in the Family" is the host of spinoff shows it inspired. First, there was "Maude" (1972–78), Edith's outspoken, upper-middle class, ultra-liberal cousin, the civility to Archie's vulgarity. Her maid, Florida Evans, begat another sitcom, "Good Times" (1974–79), starring standup great Jimmie "Kid Dy-No-Mite" Walker. The yin to their yang was yet another spinoff, "The Jeffersons" (1975–85) who were the Bunkers' next door neighbors. George was, in effect, a black Archie Bunker. These shows broke through the banality of sitcoms by illustrating life as it was rarely seen on TV . . . something like reality.

In addition to these selections, it is important to mention some other trailblazers. "Soap" (1977–81) was one of the first really controversial shows. A spoof of soap operas, it revolved around two families: the white-collared Tates and the blue-collared Campbells. The cast included Billy Crystal as one of the first homosexual characters and Robert Guillaume as Benson, the wise-cracking, surly, African-American

121

butler who later went on to big spinoff success himself. Though the show was boycotted by Moral Majority-esque groups, ABC maintained that "through the Campbells and the Tates, many of today's social concerns will be dealt with in a comedic manner."

We must also give a comedic nod to the most important spinoff of the ultra successful sitcom "Happy Days." "Joanie Loves Chachi" was in its time—Ha! Got ya! After attempting to kidnap Richie Cunningham, the alien from Ork, comedic genius Robin Williams, was given his own show, "Mork and Mindy." This weekly venue displayed a wide range of Williams's own brand of wackiness and was one of a chain of successful shows built around a comedian.

It's too soon to say what recent shows are going to fit into the big picture of sitcom history, but if we were betting types we'd put money on "The Larry Sanders Show," "Dr. Katz" and anything that doesn't feature Dabney Coleman.

Now, our favorites. The shows that did make the cut are the ones that immediately bring to mind several classic episodes—the programs that the mere mention of attracts throngs to the water cooler. Someone starts with "What do you do at a yellow light?" from the classic "Taxi" episode, and suddenly you're there for hours, sharing the common bond of TV memories.

Classic episodes should not be confused with mere reruns. Classic episodes are to reruns as Danielle Steele novels are to books written by Russian guys. They encompass what elevated the show to greatness and brought it back for more.

These shows can be found, if not in prime time, then on video or in syndication. Two classic episodes will be highlighted from each show. "The Simpsons" and "M*A*S*H" will each have three, because we had to narrow it down from a jillion.

THE MARY TYLER MOORE SHOW

Quiz question #1A—Who can turn the world on with her smile? Who can take a nothing day and suddenly make it all seem worthwhile? If you guessed Minneapolis's Mary Richards, watch your mailbox for your prize (a blue tam-o'-shanter to be thrown in the city intersection of your choice).

First airing in 1970, "The Mary Tyler Moore Show" was thought by some to be Laura Petrie's Road Not Taken. On the heels of the hayseed sitcoms "Green Acres," "Petticoat Junction" and "The Beverly Hillbillies," "The Mary Tyler More Show" was the boomerang returning. It was intelligent, modern and real. There was no occultish nose-twitching or eye-blinking. Instead you got single-career-woman-in-a-studio-apartment-with-a-fold-out-couch.

Without overblown caricatures, Mary's situations were fairly commonplace. This is probably what accounts for the show's amazing success today in syndication. A bad date hasn't changed since 1970—a lot of them even dress the same.

Aside from the relevance, there was brilliant writing and producing by James L. Brooks and Allan Burns. Brooks was fresh from creating "Room 222," though he'd go on to do quite a bit more, and Burns had written for "Get Smart." They were brought together by Moore and her then hus-

123

band, CBS executive Grant Tinker. These were probably the most important choices made.

Or maybe it was the casting, an ensemble that was unparalleled. At home were Rhoda Morgenstern (Valerie Harper) and Phyllis Lindstrom (Cloris Leachman), each of whom went on to a spinoff of her own. In the WJM newsroom were Lou Grant (Ed Asner), who had a non-comedic spinoff, pre-Captain Stubinged Gavin MacLeod as Murray Slaughter (hard to believe he was once funny) and Ted Knight as Ted Baxter. Also included were running cameos from Nancy Walker as Rhoda's mother, Nanette Fabray as Mary's mother, Betty White as Sue Ann Nivens, and Georgia Engel as Baxter's wife Georgette.

"The Mary Tyler Moore Show" endured until 1977, when it voluntarily left the air in one of the most tearful finales of all time.

"Chuckles Bites The Dust"

Chuckles the Clown, while dressed as a peanut, gets crushed to death by an elephant, prompting a nervous outbreak of black humor in the newsroom. Mary, who's been keeping it together, completely loses it at the funeral.

A breakthrough episode, "Chuckles" laughed at death but examined our sacrosanct treatment of it. David Lloyd, the writer, said that when it aired, he got the most mail not from people who had lost family or friends or any sort of humans, but pets!

"The Dinner Party"

A congresswoman unexpectedly accepts an invitation to Mary's dinner party.

Essentially about one of Mary's trademark bad dinner parties, the episode was a perfect example of how funny this cast could make an ordinary situation. Sue Ann cooks—just enough food, well, not exactly enough food. Mr. Grant takes too much and has to put it back. Rhoda brings a date, played by Henry Winkler, who is one person too many and has to sit alone at the table by the window. The episode is probably best remembered for launching Winkler's career with the priceless delivery of his one and only line.

SEINFELD

"I couldn't understand a word the cab driver said, and his name was Mumps or something! It was like an episode of "Seinfeld." "A guy knocked my cart in the supermarket and didn't say excuse me. I should write it in to "Seinfeld."

Apparently, the creators of "Seinfeld" are speaking to people—so much so that *everyone* thinks it's their life.

The show revolves around standup comic Jerry Seinfeld, who plays himself. Set on the Upper West Side of Manhattan (where he really lives when not in Los Angeles), the show's other denizens are Elaine Benes, Seinfeld's ex-girlfriend and pal, played by Julia Louis-Dreyfus, George Costanza, his neurotic best friend, played by Jason Alexander, and Kramer, his wacky next-door neighbor, played by Michael Richards. (It's interesting to note that every major member of the cast has a product endorsement contract, even George's parents!)

For as long as there have been sitcoms, there have been standup comics starring in them—Jimmy Walker, Bob Newhart, Gabe Kaplan. The refreshing aspect of "Seinfeld" is that Jerry is himself. He isn't given a TV last name or another career. The show opens and closes with cutaways to his standup routine. They even did an episode about Jerry getting his own network show. (No plans as of yet to do a show about Jerry picking up a buxom high school girl in Central Park.)

"The Outing"

Jerry is waiting to be interviewed by a reporter at the neighborhood diner, Monk's, and George is with him. Unknown to them, the reporter is sitting nearby and, overhearing George and Jerry clowning around, comes to the conclusion that they're gay. For the rest of the show, every time they try to prove they aren't, the friends get deeper into the hole.

This is a great example of taking a stock sitcom misunderstanding and really milking it. What makes it even funnier is that the characters are trying so hard to be politically correct about the whole thing. ("Not that there's anything wrong with it" is the show's catch phrase.)

"The Masturbation Episode"

This episode is about, you know. The characters never actually say the word, although they discuss it endlessly. The idea is that they're having a contest to see who can go without doing it the longest. Jerry has a hysterical rant to Kramer about "dating a virgin and seeing a naked woman (out his window) and I'm in this contest and I'm really going crazy!" Elaine is at her health club and John John Kennedy is there, and well, you know . . .

M*A*S*H

"M*A*S*H" finished its first season in forty-sixth place, and ended its run eleven years later with the single highest rated program in television history. A fitting irony for a comedy about the ravages of war.

Feature films, for the most part, do not translate well to TV. There are exceptions, though, and "M*A*S*H" is a big one. It was so successful that it surpassed the Robert Altman film, its progenitor, in popularity.

Not "Hogan's Heroes," "M*A*S*H" didn't insist you laugh. In fact, it was just as happy if you cried. The 4077th was a unit of mixed characters and extras. Some were funny, some were desperate, some were look-away-from-the-screen heartbroken. Led by Alan Alda, the Swami of Sensitive, as

127

Captain Hawkeye Pierce, you were never really sure where you might be going.

About a Mobile Army Surgical Hospital, "M*A*S*H" was a thinly veiled satire more about the (then-current) Vietnam war than Korea, where it was set. It also capitalized on the antiwar movement, but it was more than a "war is hell" show. A lot more. It was as popular with actual veterans as it was with 9-year-olds and grandmothers. It universalized a very limited experience. And it was hilarious.

Because the show had such a long life, the characters had a chance to fully evolve and grow, and we got to know them as well as our own families—from early cast members Wayne Rogers as Trapper John, McLean Stevenson as Colonel Blake and Larry Linville as Frank Burns to later and equally beloved company, Mike Farrell as B.J. Hunnicut, David Ogden Stiers as Charles Emerson Winchester and Harry Morgan as Colonel Sherman Potter. We watched Margaret Houlihan (Loretta Swit) lose the "Hot Lips" and gain sensitivity, and Corporal Klinger (Jamie Farr) lose the dress and pumps. We were perennially moved by Father Mulcahey (William Christopher) and Radar O'Reilly (Gary Burghoff).

"M*A*S*H" took television to new heights. It tackled issues from military genocide and interracial relationships to male cross dressing and managed to find humor in the most unlikely place.

"Adam's Ribs"
Disgusted by the mess tent buffet, Hawkeye radios an order to his favorite Chicago barbecue joint—for forty pounds of ribs . . . to go.

A very funny episode that managed not to be about war. In fact, the battles took a back seat. It was great fun being swept up in the escape fantasy and the silliness.

"The Interview"
A season finale. Shot in black and white, documentary style, real life war correspondent Clete Roberts interviews the men and women of the 4077th about their lives.

One of the starkest hours of "comedy" history, scripted as well as improvised questions were given to the cast members for chilling results. This show was written and directed by "M*A*S*H" creator Larry Gelbart, who left the series after this episode.

"Preventative Medicine"

Hawkeye performs an unnecessary appendectomy on a callous colonel to take him out of commission. It is his hope that the surgery will prevent the colonel from taking more boys to the front, where he could care less about their welfare. B.J. takes issue with that kind of "preventative medicine."

An episode that is less funny than it is thought-provoking, it was the result of the same argument between Mike Farrell and Alan Alda. In the original script, both doctors colluded on the operation, but after the two became embroiled in a heated argument, the storyline was changed.

THE BOB NEWHART SHOW

Mary Tyler Moore was sort of the bubbly, head cheerleader, homecoming queen to Bob Newhart's quiet captain of the chess club. He did more than fine, but never quite received his much deserved accolades in his classmate's sizable shadow.

Of course, had it not been for the success of Mary's show, Bob might never have gotten his. It was CBS's attempt to make lightning strike twice. Lorenzo Music and David Davis, Mary's crackshot writer/producer team, were given free rein—design a sitcom of your choosing around whomever you wish. In unison they cried "Bob Newhart!" but had a little trouble coming up with a premise. Holed up in Santa Barbara, they created a pilot (choosing Bob's profession as a psychologist by flipping through a phone book), and waited for Newhart's approval. He had declined many past proposals, but this script was so good, he couldn't refuse.

Though the choice of profession was somewhat arbitrary, nothing could have been more perfect. The "Button Down" comic made his name with enormously entertaining onstage phone calls—Newhart had a remarkably funny method of listening. What better occupation could there be? In addition, a psychologist could be the catalyst for a steady flow of loony patients.

Though Bob Hartley's patients were wacky, a wonderful group that included Jack Riley (as Mr. Carlin), Florida Friebus, John Fiedler, Noam Pitlik and Howard Hesseman, his co-workers were even kookier. Jerry the dentist (Peter Bonerz) and Carol the receptionist (Marcia Wallace) provided marvelous foils for the well adjusted, very Catholic, ex-accountant. At home was next-door neighbor Howard Borden (Bill Daily from "I Dream of Jeannie"), who was positively surreal.

But normalcy could be found! She was in the form of Bob's wife, Emily (Suzanne Pleshette), a smart, sexy, sharp woman (W-O-M-A-N, I'll say it again). They were older than thirty, they didn't have kids, they had sex. This was the seventies!

"Death of a Fruitman"

Mr. Gianelli, an abrasive member of Bob's therapy group, is crushed to death when a load of zucchini falls on him. The group members, who hated him in life, lionize him in death, and Bob has to make them see that he was still who he was, cruel fate or not.

The best episodes of "Bob Newhart" were the ones revolving around that great group. This episode was particularly interesting because of its resemblance in theme to "Chuckles Bites the Dust" on "The Mary Tyler Moore Show."

"Over the River and Through the Woods"

Emily goes home alone for Thanksgiving, leaving Bob to make the best of it with Jerry, Howard and Mr. Carlin.

The bachelors end up spending the day soused. They order in Chinese food and watch football. Bob does one of the best drunk bits ever. This episode's just plain silly and hysterical.

TAXI

When Elaine Nardo (Marilu Henner) comes to drive at The Sunshine Cab Company, she tells Alex Reiger (Judd Hirsch) that she is only working there part-time and temporarily. You see, *she* is a receptionist in an art gallery. "Oh yeah, I know," Alex reponds knowingly, "We're all part-timers. See that guy over there? Now he's an actor. The guy on the phone, he's a prize fighter. This lady over here, she's a beautician. The man behind her, he's a writer. Me? I'm a cab driver. I'm the only cab driver in this place." Oddly enough, by accepting who he was, Alex distinguished himself from the other drivers. He became The Sunshine Cab Company Sage, Guardian and Champion.

"Taxi" was the result of efforts by MTM alumni Ed Weinberger, Stan Daniels, David Davis and James L. Brooks. With "Taxi," they arrived at a new level.

ATHLETES WHO CROSSED OVER TO COMEDY ACTING

Kareem Abdul Jabar, *Airplane*

Muggsy Bogues, *Forget Paris*

O.J. Simpson, *Naked Gun*

Alex Karras, *Webster*

George Foreman, *George*

Bob Uecker, *Mr. Belvedere*

Bubba Smith, *Police Academy*

Not about professionals or artists, "Taxi" was set in a garage and followed the lives of New York City cab drivers and their despotic dispatcher. Where "Mary Tyler Moore" and "Bob Newhart" were about the comfortable middle class, "Taxi"'s characters were more working class. Unlike bus driver Ralph Kramden and sewer worker Ed Norton, though, the cabbies didn't spout words that sounded like they were written by a team of gag writers.

"Taxi" got the axe not once, but two times, from two different networks. First it was canceled by ABC, then before HBO grabbed it, NBC jumped in. The head of NBC at the time was Grant Tinker. (Incidentally, he was also the president of MTM when "Taxi"'s creators, MTM defectors, wanted to buy the rights to the "Taxi" story, owned by MTM. Tinker sold it to them for fifteen hundred dollars, exactly what he paid for it.) The men were interested in the story because it was about guys—they had written for the single career woman long enough. And guys they got! In addition to Hirsch, there was Bobby Wheeler (Jeff Conaway), Louie DePalma (Danny DeVito), Jim Ignatowski (Christopher Lloyd), Tony Banta (Tony Danza), and Latka Gravas (Andy Kaufman). The first season there was also John (J. Randall Carver). The only women were Elaine and, later, Latka's wife Simka (Carol Kane).

So they had been saved, but not forever. As classy, smart, and witty as it was, "Taxi" just couldn't prevail. Thankfully, though, it is currently enjoying a long, healthy afterlife in syndication.

"Paper Marriage"

Latka marries a call girl to obtain U.S. citizenship. The ceremony is presided over by the Reverend Jim Ignatowski, who after this episode became a permanent cast member.

As a tale of the disillusioning of the immigrant in America, the episode was almost a metaphor for the whole series. After the wedding, the hooker thanks him, strips off her wedding dress, grabs her cash and takes off. Latka sighs, "Boy, America is a tough town." The episode fully illustrated how this assortment of blue-collar friends could band together and find a little identity and peace in the world.

"The Great Line"

Also about an unusual wedding, this episode has John developing second thoughts after marrying a girl he met in Mario's the night before.

One of the series's single best scenes is in "The Great Line." Alex accompanies John to his new in-laws to explain just how it is their daughter married a guy she met only hours before. Dolph Sweet, as the girl's father, tells Alex that love at first sight is "a debasement of everything I and my family hold dear."

THE ODD COUPLE

"The Odd Couple" has had more incarnations than Michael Jackson's face. It's been a feature film, an album, a play—twice, (once with men, once with women)—a television series, also twice (Caucasian and African American) and a cartoon (a neat cat and a sloppy dog). But of all of Neil Simon's adverse duos, one prevailed, lasting thirteen years and gaining immortality in syndication. The Neat Cat and the Sloppy Dog! No, no, no. Of course it was Jack Klugman and Tony Randall.

Felix Unger and Oscar Madison have become the Sultans of Syndication. More than characters, they are icons of modern anti-buddyism, thriving on their opposition.

In addition to Neil Simon, the creative minds behind "The Odd Couple" were Garry Marshall and Jerry Belson. Marshall had written for "The Dick Van Dyke Show" and would go on to do "Mork and Mindy," "Happy Days," and "Laverne and Shirley" before becoming a leading motion picture director (*Pretty Woman* to name one of his films). Belson had also worked on "The Dick Van Dyke Show" and would go on to screenwrite

Smile, The End and *Fun With Dick and Jane.* Together they created the unique atmosphere of a three-camera setup and a live audience.

Supporting Randall and Klugman were Marshall's sister Penny as Myrna Turner, Oscar's secretary, Al Molinaro as Murray the Cop and Elinor Donahue as Miriam.

Sitcoms are usually set in either a home or a workplace. Most have a little of both, but one predominates. Usually the ones set in the home revolve around a family. "The Odd Couple" is no different.

Felix and Oscar are two divorced men who have decided to room together. What they don't realize is that they are entering into another "marriage." Because of the gender switch, they actually get away with a lot more than a "normal" couple would. Felix can nag Oscar to clean up after himself or to call if he's going to be late for dinner without being accused of sexist stereotyping. They were one of the first non-traditional family units to be seen on TV. Each week we would tune in to see them answer the question: Can two divorced men share an apartment without driving each other crazy?

"A Grave for Felix"

Oscar gambles away the money Felix has entrusted him for his grave site.

Another funny take on death, this episode has Felix fussing over the positions in which his loved ones will stand when they come to visit his tombstone. Oscar, in his usual laid-back manner, uses Felix's urn as an ashtray.

At the grave sight, Oscar observes an adjoining plot:

"Split Carson: beloved husband, devoted father, never threw a gutterball."

"Felix Remarries"
Felix, promising that he has mended his finicky ways, re-marries Gloria. This is the last show of the series.

A nice but not overly sentimental episode, it perfectly tied up the show, as well as provided a nice little coda.

At the end of the program, Felix thanks Oscar, and with a hearty, "I salute you," dumps a basket of garbage on the floor. "You know how I'm going to salute you?" Oscar asks. "I'm going to clean that up." Felix smiles, "It hasn't been in vain." And leaves. Oscar looks at the mess and says, "I'm not going to clean that up." And off to his room he goes. The front door opens again. "I knew he wouldn't clean that up," says Felix, who does. Perfect.

THE SIMPSONS

The only difference between "The Simpsons" and other family sitcoms is that "The Simpsons" are animated and yellow, while other sitcom families are real and flesh-colored. At least that's what they want you to think. Then you won't realize what's really going on. "The Simpsons" is the most subversive, anarchic show on TV.

Shrouded in family sitcom clichés, (like the dumb, oafish well-meaning Dad who spends nights at the local tavern) "The Simpsons" fools you into thinking it's much more ordinary than it is. This is not Fred and Wilma, Claire and Cliff, Herman and Lily, or even Peggy and Al.

Begining as a sketch on The Fox Network's "The Tracey

ATHLETES WHO'VE BEEN ON "THE SIMPSONS"

Steve Sax

Jose Canseco

Ken Griffey, Jr.

Mike Scoscia

Ozzie Smith

Darryl Strawberry

Don Mattingly

Ullman Show," "The Simpsons" evolved from a colorful punch line to an insanely clever and thought-provoking commentary on modern society. It is the product of cartoonist Matt Groening, who loosely based it on his own clan and set it in the Anytown, USA of "Springfield." It caused quite a commotion from the start. Bart Simpson T-shirts were outlawed in schools (like "Underachiever and Proud of It" and "I'm Bart Simpson, who the hell are you?") and parents were outraged at his unpenalized antics.

It was scary, and no one was safe. Especially authority. The cast of fools include Police Chief Wiggum, Principal Skinner, teacher Mrs. Krabappel and news anchor Kent Brockman.

The tweaks on clichés include Homer, the dad—he works at a plant . . . a nuclear power plant! His boss, Mr. Burns, has a male secretary, Smithers, who has a crush on

Burns (and an extensive Malibu Stacy doll collection.) The wacky neighbor is a syrupy, good-hearted Christian, Ned Flanders, whose kids, even worse, play a board game called "Good Samaritan." Bart and Lisa Simpson love to watch the very violent cartoon "Itchy and Scratchy," inspiring a show in which Marge stages a boycott of its sponsors (though this ended in a politically correct way with a nice message about the evils of censorship).

"The Simpsons's" cameo roster reads like a who's who of cameo roles. Elizabeth Taylor, Dustin Hoffman (credited as Sam Etic), Michael Jackson (credited as John Jay Smith), Jose Canseco, Michelle Pfeiffer, James Woods, Jackie Mason, Harvey Fierstein, and Aerosmith, to name a few.

Because at its heart there's a good, loving family and a solid story line, "The Simpsons" reaches young and old alike. Children and adults each manage to find their own place in the blue-collar family with the blue-haired mom.

It is hard to narrow down "The Simpson's" best episodes, each choice bringing about "Oh yeah, I loved that one, but remember the one with the dental plan where Lisa plays "Classical Gas" . . . well, we tried.

"A Streetcar Named Desire"

The community theater of Springfield puts on a musical version of *A Streetcar Named Desire*, with Ned Flanders as Stanley Kowalski. Jon Lovitz is the play's flamboyant director.

Encompassing what is best about the series, the "Streetcar" episode has a basic family problem and a good story— Homer isn't paying enough attention to Marge. But it is surrounded by perfect material, including a parody of *The*

Great Escape with Maggie in a nursery school run by the Lovitz character's sister.

"The Country Singer"

Homer decides to manage a country singer he hears in an out-of-town cowboy bar.

Beverly D'Angelo is Lurleen Lumpkin, the guest voice of the week. She falls in love with Homer, and in the end he decides he must leave her to be with Marge and the kids. Lots of good jokes and that nice illustration of family values, Simpson style.

"Dancin' Homer"

Homer, after dancing on the dugout at the company outing, is asked to be the Springfield Isotopes' team mascot. He proudly tells Marge, "This ticket doesn't just give me a seat, it also gives me the right, no, the duty to make a complete ass of myself!"

Matt Groening wrote this episode, where Homer, nicknamed "Dancin' Homer," whoops it up to "Baby Elephant Walk," and goes on to the big leagues in Capital City, where he ultimately must fail.

Ex-Letterman-writer-turned-Simpson-writer Jeff Martin penned the song "Capital City," masterfully sung by none other than Tony Bennett ("There's a swingin' town I know, Capital City").

A Guide to Situation Comedy Clichés

The only way you get any feeling out of your television set is if you touch it when you're wet.
—Larry Gelbart

Situation comedy: the very term is comforting, like a pair of old holey pajamas that you just don't want to part with. And it's that very comfort that forces us to discuss the sitcom here in this chapter.

If there's any one kind of comedy that feeds on its own clichés and conventions, it's the situation comedy. Somebody once said there are really only six stories. Maybe they said five, or seven, we're not sure. It doesn't matter. It seems that sitcom writers have found them and keep telling them over and over again. Sometimes they tell them with Suzanne Pleshette, sometimes (too often really) with the late Bill Bixby.

We'll point out some of those conventions, the contrivances to watch for when you settle in for a night of reruns. As far as we're concerned, the bulk of these stories are representative of an off-week in the writers' room. Rarely are there any real surprises in them. They're simply gimmicks on which to hang a few gags.

THE TRAPPED IN SOME KIND OF SMALL ROOM EPISODE

Could be a meat locker, storage room, cellar, whatever. It's a small area in which the characters can reveal something deep and touching to each other. When Mike and Archie end up in the storage room at Archie's bar on "All in the Family," Mike learns that his father-in-law was taunted as a child for wearing one shoe and one boot to school. When Bobby and Greg end up trapped in Sam the Butcher's meat locker on "The Brady Bunch," Bobby learns that being short is okay, because he can fit through the window and free them from the locker. On "The Bob Newhart Show," Bob and Emily end up locked in their cellar and miss their own Bicentennial party. All they learned, though, was how annoyed their friends were that they missed their own party.

THE DREAM/FANTASY EPISODE

Usually seen four or five seasons into a series' run, when most other plots have been exhausted, this episode allows the writers to discard all the standard formulas for the show and let their imaginations run wild. On "The Mary Tyler Moore Show," Lou, Murray and Ted fantasized about being married to Mary. "The Dick Van Dyke Show" had Rob dream that the world was being overrun with walnuts and taken over by Danny Thomas. Bob Hartley dreamed of a date with Morgan Fairchild. The thing that's often a cheat with dream episodes is that you almost never see the character who's dreaming actually fall asleep. It's only when the character wakes up that the viewer realizes that it's a dream.

THE "SCROOGE" EPISODE

One character, who hates Christmas, assumes the role of Ebenezer Scrooge. On "The Odd Couple," it was Oscar. On "Family Ties," it was Alex. If Dickens were around today, he'd be making a fine living doing scripts for "Murphy Brown."

THE "WHAT WE'LL LOOK LIKE WHEN WE'RE 70" EPISODE

This is the one where the makeup people cut loose. The characters imagine what life will be like when they're 70 years old. Series as diverse as "The Mary Tyler Moore Show," "Saved by the Bell," "Cheers," and "Family Matters" have hauled out the prosthetics and let the cast play dress-up. This episode is closely related to the "Regular Cast Member Playing His or Her Own Grandparent," which was part of such comedies as "The Brady Bunch" and "The Odd Couple."

THE RETROSPECTIVE EPISODE

This is the one where the cast members sit around and talk about all the great times they've had, which are illustrated with clips from past episodes. It gives the writers a chance to turn in about three minutes of script for a twenty-two-minute show. Often, the episode is predicated on some monumental event taking place, such as a birth or the sale of a house ("Fresh Prince of Bel Air"). Occasionally, the producers will mix two overused ideas by pairing this concept with that of "Trapped in a Small Room." Instead of revealing insights, the characters toss around "Remember that time?" stories. The record holder for the retrospective episode is "Family Ties," which had not one, not two, not even three, but *four* retrospectives of the ups and downs of the Keaton family. Did that much exciting stuff happen to those people that we had to relive it four times?

THE "GOING ON TELEVISION" EPISODE

Series such as "The Mary Tyler Moore Show" and "Murphy Brown" are about television professionals, but many other series have produced episodes in which the characters appear on television. Somehow, though, the characters almost always appear on television *live.* Consequently, some kind of misunderstanding or revelation can occur in front of millions of people. On "The Bob Newhart Show," Bob appeared live on a talk show with a woman who seemed perfectly nice off camera, but when the red light went on trashed the entire practice of psychology. When the kids on "The Brady Bunch" appeared on Hal Sterne's Amateur Hour, which for some reason was broadcast live, Mom, Dad and Alice found out that they were singing and dancing to raise money to buy their folks an anniversary gift. When Felix and Oscar embarrassed themselves on David Steinberg's late night talk show on "The Odd Couple," it never occurred to anyone to edit them out of the show, because it was live. The truly ironic part of all this is that all the shows on which this live broadcasting occurred were, in fact, on tape. In fact, a study showed that the amount of live broadcasting that goes on in TV is far higher than that which occurs in real life.

THE "MAKEOVER" EPISODE

This is the one where a character who formerly couldn't put together a complete sentence becomes scholarly and mannered, or a nebbish suddenly becomes sexy and attractive—all in the first five minutes of the episode. The producers of "Taxi" used this one over an entire season by giving Andy Kaufman's Latka multiple personalities. This allowed him to go from being the lovable immigrant to a womanizing, accent-free stud named Vic Ferrari. On "Family Matters," Urkel used a magic transformation machine (yes, a magic transformation machine) that turned him into the devastatingly handsome Stephan Urquelle. And, on "Family Ties," Alex undertook the task of transforming Mallory's boyfriend Nick from a leather-jacketed grease monkey to a smoking-jacketed intellectual. This is truly one of the more insulting conceits for producers to shovel at the audience. It goes beyond suspending disbelief and into the realm of magic transformation machines (yes, magic transformation machines).

Of course, if you're a viewer of situation comedy, you know that these conventions and others run rampant throughout the form. The next time you're watching something and the producers try to slide one of these lame-o concepts past you, think of this chapter and remember that you'd serve yourself better spending the half hour cutting your nails. Or someone else's, if that's your cup of tea.

Open Mikers:
Dave Attell

Dave Attell was not the class clown. "I sat behind him," the Long Island-born comedian says dryly.

Attell never wanted to become a comic. Even after Attell was doing it, he wasn't that sure. "It took me a couple of years before I actually decided that this was what I was going to be." It's a lucky thing, too, because the only alternate career he could come up with is "bounty hunter."

Attell admits to falling into his vocation. It all started when he was a New York University film student ("I hated it.") Hanging out at comedy clubs, he began courting the open mike. "I worked the door at the old Improvisation. They threw me on late at night," he recalls,

"I temped and waited tables for money. Then I started getting paid for standup, and the rest is history."

One of four children, Attell is encouraged by his parents. "I guess they sort of want me to be like Seinfeld—that's their idea of a comic," he says. "But they don't care, as long as I keep sending them the checks."

As a comic, Attell travels quite a bit. It just all happens to be within Manhattan. Working at as many as eight clubs in one night in various parts of the city, Attell is at it seven nights a week. If he could get frequent flyer mileage for his cab fare, he'd have a round trip ticket to Bangkok by now.

When not performing or sleeping, Attell works as a writer (he wrote for "SNL" and the now defunct "Jon Stewart Show.") He was also, along with standup greats Dom Irrera and Ray Romano, a first-season patient of Dr. Katz's, a gig you don't get unless you're at the top of your game.

If you only know Attell from his Letterman appearances, you probably see him as a nebbishy Jewish guy from Long Island dressed in a blazer, hair combed—he could easily be an accountant—someone who'd choke on a cigarette. If, however, you're lucky enough to have seen him perform at one of his New York haunts, like the Comedy Cellar in Greenwich Village, he'd be the last guy you'd want filing your 1040s.

His live show is bluer than his network sets, and Attell, a bit paunchy, dresses in his clothes from the 'hood—a leather jacket, jeans and high tops, backwards baseball hat, and a never-ending chain of smokes. He is edgy, sometimes explosive, even a bit scary, but not in a Manson way. More like an Andy Kaufman way. He could make you laugh till your guts hurt, or he could blow up in your face.

Currently single, Attell appears not to have enough time in the day for a social life, "I was on a date with this really hot model," he tells the audience. "Play along, all right?" They laugh. "Anyway, it wasn't really a *date* date, we just ate dinner, saw a movie, then the plane landed."

Long range, Attell wants to be what he is, just better at it. "I really like doing standup. I know you can't do it forever," he admits. "I just think it's the coolest thing you can do. No responsibility to anyone but yourself."

VARIATIONS

ON A JOKE

Among those whom I like or admire, I can find no common denominator, but among those whom I love, I can: all of them make me laugh.

—W. H. Auden

Every comic will acknowledge that comedy is about style. It's about delivery. It's about inflection. It's about taking a beat before hitting the audience with the punch line. It's about timing. It's about how different comics tell the same joke differently.

On his album, "Mind Over Matter," Robert Klein parodied a fifties Borscht Belt comic who set up jokes in English, then paid them off with Yiddish punch lines. The point of the routine was that comics all tell the same handful of jokes, but each one tailors them for specific audiences. Consider this joke, which you might have heard if you were a guest at a Catskills hotel in the fifties:

> Two business partners take a trip to Florida. Just as they get seated on the train, one of them jumps up and screams "My God! I left the safe open!" The other

partner shrugs his shoulders and replies "*Wus deigst die? Ins sennen beider du, nicht?*"*

Now, of course, this joke is about as old as jokes get, but even such a tired gag as this is still being used in ways that make it fresh for different audiences.

The joke comes from a book that was published in 1938, and the joke was old then. In fact, there's a possibility that this gag, or some variation of it, might be part of an ancient Roman comedy. But that doesn't mean that it can't still work. How could that joke be made contemporary? Think about the last time you watched a sitcom with two characters who are adversaries, but deep down really love, or at least like each other. Can't think of any? What about Urkel and

---

*"We're both here, aren't we?" The Yiddish punch line is what audiences would hear at a Jewish mountain resort like Kutsher's. The idea of telling jokes in English with a foreign punch line gave audiences the feeling that the material was tailored to them, and in some ways it was. Jewish comics casually tossed references to kosher food or Jewish traditions into their acts.

There's a good chance this joke made it off the boat with the immigrants in the early part of this century. The next logical place for it would have been the Yiddish theater in the Jewish ghettos in Manhattan. From there, working its way north to the Catskills would have been almost unavoidable, as many of the comics who ended up working the mountains grew up in those ghettos.

New York's Jewish neighborhoods have long been considered a breeding ground for comedy. In the early part of the century, Russian and Polish Jews fled persecution and settled in bustling neighborhoods on the Lower East Side and in Upper Manhattan. Among the comics who found humor in the conditions they endured there in their childhoods are the Marx Brothers, Henny Youngman, George Burns and Eddie Cantor. There was something about the combination of old-world traditions with immigrant ambitiousness that made New York a training ground for many industries, but it's most famous for the comedians it has launched.

This is the only footnote in the book and it's here simply so the authors could say they put one in.

Carl on "Family Matters?" Or Lou Grant and Ted Baxter on "The Mary Tyler Moore Show"?

What about "The Dick Van Dyke Show," in which Mel Cooley and Buddy Sorrell constantly antagonized one another? Mel's officiousness and bald head were the only things Buddy needed to keep Mel slow burning, day after day. Imagine a situation in which Mel and Buddy had to keep secret from Alan Brady a sketch that Rob has written.

MEL: Rob wont be back from vacation for another three days.

BUDDY: So?

MEL: So Alan can't find out about the gypsy fortune teller sketch until Rob gets here. Suppose somebody tells him.

BUDDY: What are you worried about? We're both here, aren't we?

See that? The same joke. Two guys who don't trust each other but are forced to work together. It's really a matter of context. It's determining who tells the joke and who hears it. What if you were attending a convention of dentists? (That is, if you're a dentist. If not, please leave the exhibit hall immediately.) Think about someone bombastic and verbose like Alan King playing at the opening dinner. How would the joke play there?

My dentists: Dr. Gold and Dr. Jacobs. The office door says "Two Jews and a Spit Sink." I see them once a year when my wife, the Floss Queen, starts wondering how much longer she'll be able to eat corn on the cob.

I'm sitting in the chair and my mouth is filled with enough cotton to knit a sweater for Dom DeLuise and they're discussing a brand-new plaque pick they've designed. I can tell the novocaine's taking effect because they're not nearly as annoying as they usually are. So they're talking about this plaque pick and Gold says, "I left the plans for the pick in the downstairs office. What if somebody steals it?" And Jacobs says, "What are you worried about? We're both here, aren't we? You can spit now, Mr. King."

A guy like Alan King shapes the joke to the audience, but also gives it his own personal touches. He turns a hoary two-liner into a story with characters and atmosphere. From the way he tells the joke, you get the sense that he's been seeing Gold and Jacobs for years. The oldest joke in the world becomes a true story if King tells you it is.

Consider somebody like Bob Newhart, whose material could never be mistaken for true stories. Newhart's standup act consisted of his end of telephone conversations with people like Sir Walter Raleigh or Abe Lincoln. He could make this joke play too, if he were on a conference call with the Wright brothers.

Hi, Wilbur, Orville . . . you guys both there? You were out back with the what? The airplane? Oh, that flying thing . . . listen, guys, I'm calling about that new wing design you were telling me about. That's right, the one with the picture of your mom on it . . . what's that, Orville? You're . . . you're afraid somebody's going to steal the wing design from you guys. Well, I don't

---

MISTER MOVIE TITLES:

Mr. Ace

Mr. Billion

Mr. Destiny

Mr. Dynamite

Mr. Hex

Mr. Love

Mr. Lucky

Mr. Majestyk

Mr. Mom

Mr. Music

Mr. Rock and Roll

Mr. Soft Touch

Mr. Superinvisible

Mr. Wise Guy

---

think you have anything to worry about, I mean you're both there, aren't you? Orville? Wilbur? You guys still there? Thought I lost you. You're . . . you're right, that really isn't that funny . . . what's that, Orville? Do I think you should be able to get from Kitty Hawk to Charlotte without having to stop in Raleigh? Sure, I guess so . . . Wilbur thinks you need a layover? Why's that, Wilbur? You . . . you have to put more of those little bottles of vodka on the airplane? I see . . .

Newhart, whose style is as quiet and reactive as King's is loud and abrasive, would have shaped the joke to fit credibly within the context of his standup act. And he would have done it simply by adding a few scene-setting details before and after the gag itself.

THE BEST LAWYER JOKES EVER

An engineer, a physicist, and a lawyer were being interviewed for a position as president of a large corporation. The engineer was interviewed first and was asked a long list of questions, ending with "How much is two plus two?" The engineer left the room and made a series of measurements and calculations. When he returned to the boardroom he said, "Four."

The physicist was interviewed next and was asked the same questions. Before answering the last question, he excused himself, headed over to the library, and did a great deal of research. After a consultation with the United States Bureau of Standards and many calculations, he also announced "Four."

The lawyer was interviewed last, and was asked the same questions. At the end of his interview, before answering the last question, he drew all the shades in the room, looked outside the door to see if anyone was there, checked the telephone for listening devices, and asked "How much do you want it to be?"

An attorney died and found himself in heaven, but was not at all happy with his accommodations. He complained to St. Peter, who told him that his only recourse was to appeal his assignment.

The attorney immediately advised that he intended to appeal, but was then told that he would have to wait at least three years before his appeal could be heard. The attorney protested that a three-year wait was unconscionable, but his words fell on deaf ears. The lawyer was then approached by the devil, who told him that he would be able to arrange an appeal to be heard in a few days, if the attorney was willing to change his venue to Hell. When the attorney asked why appeals could be heard so much sooner in Hell, he was told, "We have all of the judges."

For three years, a young attorney had been taking his brief vacations at this country inn. The last time he'd finally managed an affair with the innkeeper's daughter. Looking forward to an exciting few days, he dragged his suitcase up the stairs of the inn, then stopped short. There sat his lover with an infant on her lap! "Helen, why didn't you write when you learned you were pregnant?" he cried. "I would have rushed up here, we could have gotten married, and the baby would have my name!" "Well," she said, "when my folks found out about my condition, we sat up all night talkin' and talkin' and decided it would be better to have a illegitimate grandchild in the family than a lawyer."

While Mr. Smith was on his deathbed, he attempted to formulate a plan that would allow him to take at least some of his considerable wealth with him. He called for the three men he trusted most—his lawyer, his doctor, and his clergyman. He told them, "I'm going to give you each $30,000 in cash before I die. At my funeral, I want you to place the money in my coffin so that I can try to take it with me." All three agreed to do this and were given the money.

At the funeral, each approached the coffin in turn and placed an envelope inside. While riding in the limousine to the cemetery, the clergyman said, "I have to confess something to you fellows. Brother Smith was a good churchman all his life, and I know he would have wanted me to do this. The church needed a new baptistery very badly, and I took $10,000 of the money he gave me and bought one. I only put $20,000 in the coffin." The physician then said, "Well, since we're confiding in one another, I might as well tell you that I didn't put the full $30,000 in the coffin either. Smith had a disease that could have been diagnosed sooner if I had this new machine, but the machine cost $20,000 and I couldn't afford it then. I used $20,000 of the money to buy the machine so that I might be able to save another patient. I know that Smith would have wanted me to do that."

The lawyer then said, "I'm ashamed of both of you. When I put my envelope into that coffin, it held my personal check for the full $30,000."

Having died, a lawyer found himself with the devil in a room filled with clocks. Each clock turned at a different speed and was labeled with the name of a different occupation. After examining all of the clocks, the lawyer turned to the devil and said, "I have two questions. First, why does each clock move at a different speed?" The devil replied, "They turn at the rate at which that occupation sins on the earth. What is your second question?" The lawyer asked where the attorneys' clock was, as he couldn't find it. The devil looked puzzled, then his face brightened and he replied, "Oh, we keep that one in the workshop. It's used as a fan."

One morning at their law office, one attorney looked at the other and said, "Wow, you look really terrible this morning." The other lawyer replied, "Yeah, I woke up with a headache this morning and, no matter what I try, I can't seem to get rid of it." The first lawyer told him, "Whenever I get a headache like that, I take a few hours off during the day, go home, and make love to my wife. Works every time for me." Later that afternoon, the two lawyers met again. The first told the second, "You know, you look 100 percent better." The second replied, "Yeah, that was great advice you gave me. You've got a beautiful house, too."

Open Mikers:
Darrell Hammond

In the early part of his career, Darrell Hammond logged a lot of miles on the highways of Florida as a kind of mobile comic. "I was living in Orlando and I found that there were open mike nights in five or six cities all over the state and I would get in my car and drive to a different one every night. I would do five minutes onstage in West Palm Beach, then the next night I'd go to Tampa, then Cocoa Beach, Orlando, Daytona."

Darrell Hammond

Though he had to supplement his comedy career with a day job, Darrell had graduated from the standard standup vocations of slinging hash and mixing martinis with work that actually allowed him to perform. "I was working at Disney World and Sea World, doing animation voices for the theme parks. I voiced characters in the parks and on commercials. I was also doing characters on morning radio shows that were on about ten stations around the country."

Darrell considered comedy "a lark," and was happy with the voice work he was doing. But after his first set went "freakishly well," he was hooked. Of course, Darrell soon found out that when you do well your first time, you're not really prepared for the first time you bomb. But he remembers what it was like. "I played one club where three hundred people didn't even look at me. They were drinking. They were mating. There were sports playing on giant televisions. My appearance had been sprung upon them. And in order to get paid, I had to pretend that they were paying attention to me, which they weren't. I did 45 minutes. It was horrible. You can't do comedy in a brothel. It reminded me of something that Woody Allen once said: 'The audience has to know they're an audience and that they're expected to laugh.' You can't imagine how many bar owners think they can simply put a microphone in a room and now it's a comedy club."

Eventually, the hell gigs of the southeast paid off, affording Darrell the opportunity to move north to New York in early 1992. But playing the country's comedy capital made Darrell feel like an open miker again. "I was roundly, completely, hideously turned away from every club in the city for almost a year and a half."

Darrell acknowledges that the difficulty he faced making it in New York has had a major affect on the way he views the business of comedy. And it's not necessarily positive.

"When you see people who just walk into the city and boom, they're onstage, it affects you. I remember when I first came to New York, there were comics who were polite to me. But there was also a sense of 'Look, we paid our dues. You will too.' I feel that now, when I see new comics come in. I'm thinking, 'Hey, pal, I bled through the ears and so did everyone here.' And it's not fair to think that way and I feel ashamed of it sometimes."

It's this kind of thinking, Darrell feels, that intensifies the feeling of competition among standups. "It probably is about as competitive as it might be in athletes trying out for a team. You have to remember that you're playing for some really big prizes: an agent for college gigs, a film agent, a TV agent." And it's not like the prizes are won and the contest is over. "Ultimately, you never really stop competing. So comics develop a gentlemen's agreement among each other. I don't mind being competitive with other comics. Just don't screw me out of a job."

Darrell is equally pragmatic about his aspirations beyond standup comedy. "I go through periods where I want to be a standup philosopher and give my views on mankind," he says. "That's fine, but if the audience isn't laughing, I have to remember that my job is to tell jokes. The ultimate, for me, would be to write something that is socially relevant and funny."

Relevance combined with comedy is something that Darrell feels he hasn't achieved yet. "I think I approximate what ten different cultures find funny and bring it onstage with me. Richard Pryor is really a hero of mine and he could talk about anything with an audience, really make it universal. And he'd find a way to make it funny."

Finding a way to make it funny for the audience is a mandate Darrell takes seriously. "I once heard Jay Leno say 'You'll never disprove the audience's value system and make them laugh.' If you're making them laugh, you're proving what is already true to them."

Darrell proved to himself the accuracy of Leno's insight during what he calls "the most exciting seven minutes" of his life: a set at Harlem's Apollo Theater in New York. "The greatest part of it was that the audience was all black and I was white. We were from completely different cultures and we had some common ground. We both found the same stuff funny. And people had warned me that I would be booed offstage; not because I was white, but because that's what the people do there. So I went onstage like I was approaching the gallows. It's one thing not to do well, but to get booed off? And there was never even a hint of that. I went on and did the tightest seven I ever did."

The fact that the Apollo is a theater rather than a night-club was a huge revelation for Darrell, because spending night after night on club stages tends to wear down even the sharpest standup. Simply, the rules are different than in a theater. "It's all those nights when you have twenty people standing in front of the stage talking while they wait to go to the bathroom. You don't have twenty people talking during *Phantom of the Opera.* You don't have a phone ringing during *Phantom of the Opera.* You don't have a blender going. None of that happens in the theater. And there are some clubs where that goes on every night and after a while, you get tired of having your punch lines trampled on by a blender."

Despite the tedium of performing in clubs, Darrell has

no intention of leaving the spotlight. "Generally, I absolutely love what I do for a living. But I'm much more conscious now of trying to improve and I guess what's happening now is it's becoming a bit more of a job. And there's nothing wrong with that. That probably means I'm just pushing harder to get better."

Of course, even the roughest standup gig isn't as tough as Darrell's current assignment: performing as a regular on "Saturday Night Live." Producer Lorne Michaels brought Darrell to the late-night TV comedy show to perform his dead-on impressions of everyone from Phil Donahue to Jesse Jackson.

Ask Darrell how he feels about the job many performers dream of and he says, "I feel very lucky." Then he adds, "Lately."

Comedy 101 Meets in the Large Lecture Hall

Wit is so shining a quality that everybody admires it; most people aim at it, all people fear it, and few love it unless in themselves.

—Lord Chesterfield

For a professional comedy writer, writing for the campus humor magazine is what playing college football is to the pro-football player. At the humor magazine, staffers are subject to random drug tests, are allowed to skip classes after producing a particularly stellar issue, and pat each other on the behinds.

Please note: This is college humor. You will find mixed in with the "whoopee diaphragm" ads references to obscure, French anarchists and underground poets. Basically you're seeing an exhibit of the only time you'd ever use the stuff you learned in college.

THE PLAGUE (NEW YORK UNIVERSITY)

A younger member of the college humor magazine family, *The Plague* was founded in 1977 and named after the disease that killed tens of thousands buried in Washington Square

---

WELL-KNOWN PEOPLE WHO WORKED AT THE *HARVARD LAMPOON*

Writer and dilettante George Plimpton

Twin comedy writers Steve O'Donnell and Mark O'Donnell

Novelist John Updike

Philosopher George Santayana

Writer for Letterman and "The Simpsons," Jeff Martin

Writer for "Saturday Night Live" and "The Simpsons," George Meyer

Writer/Talk Show Host Conan O'Brien

Writer Robert Benchley

Warner Bros. VP and daughter of Jim, Lisa Henson

Comedy writers Al Jean and Mike Reiss

Founders of the *National Lampoon,* Doug Kenny and Henry Beard

---

Park. (Washington Square Park is NYU's "quad," although unlike Big Ten schools, this quad has its own pushers, transvestite hookers and numbers racketeers!)

The Plague is published once a semester "if our equipment works," says Managing Editor Mike Zimmerman. He adds that contributors range from "angry friends" to "exasperated acquaintances," but that mostly the editors come up with stuff at the last minute.

All the Arabic an American Needs to Know
by Lawrence "of Arabia" Lewitinn
Volume XIV, Number 2, Spring 1991

You wake up in a cold sweat. The same nightmare that has repeated itself over and over again finished not two minutes ago. Despite your "top notch" NYU education, you were stupid enough to be in Iraq when the shit went down. Now you're a "guest" in a bomb shelter conveniently located near an Iraqi base, unable to converse intelligently with your "hosts." Suffer no more! With the help of an underground computer Bulletin Board Service and my Arabic-speaking dad, we here at Plague Control have put together this quick and handy guide.

Koul el hadretaak tekmoure.
"Whatever you say."

Shoukraan lakod tefaragni haza al moumtaaz.
"Thank you for showing me your marvelous gun."

Enami mabsout aala al ouzoumah enou asterayah aala el ard be reglayz weh edaya mafroudin.
"I am delighted to accept your kind invitation to lie down on the floor with my arms above my head and legs apart."

Enani moukable be koul al hadretak weh fe hayatak etkaal.
"I agree with everything you have ever said or thought in your life."

Enani moutacha ker weh ashhourak aala enni taazemni enani assarer fe el kabbout el sayaaretak el Maarseedes 280SL.

"It is exceptionally kind of you to allow me to travel in the trunk of your Mercedes 280SL."

Aargouk laa takaasar bidaani wa be maaroof inani akoun ba-laadi ela el wattan.
"If you will do me the great kindness of not harming my genitals, I will gladly reciprocate by betraying my country in public."

Enaani aattilak koul assami el souhafiyah alaazina gawaassiss amerricaaniah.
"I will most gladly tell you the names and addresses of many American spies posing as reporters."

El shasha el haamra aalla ennayya helwaa khaaless, ya amir.
"Why yes, the red blindfold is lovely, Your Excellency."

El esh el maffatfet filmayaa mahoul gedan-aooz el raasheta.
"The water-soaked bread crumbs are truly delicious. I must have your recipe."

Tabaan a fadaal akoon masgoon hadretak men makkoon maa Latifa Hanem.
"Truly, I would rather be a hostage to your greatly esteemed self than to spend a night upon the person of Christina Applegate."

Sachne el fool el eatani zartah fe oudani.
"Your national dish (of fava beans) will soon bring music to my ears."

Enani afadal a salem be aala eedak el shemal; meen fe hezel el behled yastamel weh raak maraheed?
"Of course I prefer to shake your left hand; after all, who uses toilet paper in this lovely country of yours?"

El Akhbar el Yom beten chelbish teezi.
"The *Washington Square News* is a little too rough to use for the cleaning of my rectum."

THE RECORD (YALE UNIVERSITY)

The Record of Yale had a proud beginning in 1872 running "light-hearted gossip and news bites," says Chairman Josh Goldfoot.

During the early part of the century, it flourished and became a rather profitable institution. At that time its content centered entirely around Yale, and world events if a Yalie was in attendance. "Jokes about butter rationing in the dining hall were big then," admits Goldfoot.

World War II claimed much of the *Record* staff, and things were not the same for a long time. Suffering from money troubles and finding itself outdated, *The Record* seemed on the way out. In 1970, Editor-In-Chief Garry Trudeau attempted to save it, to no avail, and it ceased to publish in 1971.

Sporadic rebirths and deaths took it to 1987, when it began to flourish as it does today. It counts among its alumni Hollywood mogul Brandon Tartikoff and aforementioned "Doonesbury" artist and Jane Pauley's husband, Garry Trudeau.

Frustrated Philosophers' Film Forum
Thursday at 6:59 & 12:00
SATURDAY NIGHT FEVER

We welcome back this classic retelling of Dostoevsky's examination of the Nietzschean Superman in contemporary society. John Travolta earned a much deserved Academy Award nomination playing this tragic hero, Tony Manero. Just as Raskolnikov rises above his surroundings to commit the atrocious murder, Manero believes it his privilege, no in fact, his duty to separate himself from his harrowing Brooklyneese friends to enter the promised land . . . Manhattan! In this modern-day tale of betrayal, friendship, socioeconomic status, and gyrating hips, the music guides us to see Manero become that Überman of disco-dancing, bridge-jumping, and grunting. A must-see for all!

Friday at 7:52 & 11:23 (Note the change in times)
IT'S THE GREAT PUMPKIN, CHARLIE BROWN

In this riveting tale of perpetual human tragedy, Schulz places his characters in the ultimate test of essence versus existence. While the rest of the Peanuts gang cavorts in the miscreant trick-or-treating ceremonies, stoics Linus and his disciple Sally wait all night in the pumpkin patch for their savior, the Great Pumpkin, to appear. Does perfection lie in subservience to a set of ideals or the search for happiness? Do humans create their identity, or is it served to them by gigantic pieces of fruit?

Thursday at 7:58 & 12:48
BEDTIME FOR BONZO

Social Darwinism pushed to the extreme! Can college professor and animal theorist Bonzo domesticate future President and Forgetful One Ronald Reagan? In this somber and
depressing movie which foretold many of our country's
problems in the eighties, we can only feel Bonzo's pain as
he waits for his subject to develop. They don't make them
like this anymore.

CHAPARRAL (STANFORD UNIVERSITY)

Another Old Boy press, *The Chappie* was started in 1899
and never ceased to publish during its ninety-six-year history.

A shiny, high-quality production, *The Chapparal* is published twice quarterly (full-color front and back cover). It is
twenty-four to thirty-two pages long, and the story on it
seems to be that a lot of eating (Dominoes and Taco Bell)
is involved in its production. The parents of the chappies
probably don't want to hear what else they do.

Famous chappies include Josh Weinstein (executive producer of "The Simpsons"), and Bruce Handy (senior editor
of *Time* magazine).

New Politically Correct Euphemisms
We know all too well how touchy people can be about what
you call them. So in the interest in informing the Stanford
community about what terms are currently in vogue, *The*

Chappie presents its guide to the current politically correct lingo (subject to change without notice).

- When you mean to say *Black,* what you should say is *African-American.*
- When you mean to say *Oriental,* what you should say is *Asian-American* or *Pacific Islander.*
- Someone who used to be *handicapped* is now *Physically Challenged* or *Differently Abled.*
- The term for *minorities* is now *People of Color.*
- *Women,* accordingly, are now *People of Gender.*
- *White, Anglo-Saxon Protestants* join the ranks of the downtrodden by becoming *Ethnically Deprived.*
- Your *short* friends are now *Vertically Challenged.*
- Likewise, the generally *stupid* are to be referred to as the *Mentally Challenged.*
- People who are *fat* preferred the less pejorative terms *People of Mass* or *Latitudinally Overpresent.*
- *Jocks* are *Physically Overabled* or *Mentally Challenged.*
- The *ugly* are *Aesthetically Challenged.*
- Members of the *animal* kingdom are *Chromosomally Different.*
- *Men* must shed their linguistic shackles and are henceforth known as *Myn.*
- Rather than being *dead,* those who are passed on are *Existentially Challenged.*

THE GARGOYLE (UNIVERSITY OF MICHIGAN AT ANN ARBOR)

The Gargoyle was founded in "don't quote me on this, but I'd say 1909," guesses Editor-In-Chief Andrew Lin. Michigan's humor magazine went through many permutations. For a time it was scandalously underground after being shut down in the sixties.

Written mostly by the editors, the masthead is filled with people who showed up at the first meeting and that was it. It has a circulation of ten thousand and comes out six times a year. And *all four* of its advertisers claim they've had a great response!

Some of the celebrated alumni include the former editor-in-chief, who's now an intern at Conan O'Brien and "some guy who's a famous cartoonist."

God's Letters to Children

Dear Jimmy,

So, you thought I wouldn't notice that piece of candy you took, Jimmy. "Surely," you said to yourself, "God can't be watching me all the time. He won't notice me take this one little piece of candy." Wrong, Jimmy. Dead Wrong. I know all about the candy. And that little lie you told your parents, too. I know it *all* Jimmy. I'm everywhere.

Everywhere.

The Lord.

Dear Kid,

I'm omnipotent omnipotent OMNIPOTENT.

That means I can do anything to any one at any time. I could turn your parents into vegetables—either kind. I could make your friends call you "Bullom-head." In fact, I could make that your official name—*in writing.* I could destroy your world, or I could turn you all into poorly contrived Styrofoam puppets. Or, I could make your pathetic little world into a wonderful land of sunshine and rainbows. Why don't I? NONE OF YOUR BUSINESS.

Just a reminder.

P.S. Oh, I didn't give you free will.

Dear Big Mac-Daddy,

I've been watching you recently, Mac, and I've noticed you've been hanging with a bad crowd and wearing lots of expensive clothes, and making your car jump like that. Now, we'll just pretend I don't know where all that new income is coming from, long as you're not breaking any laws. That would include the Law of Tithes, Mac. A lot of people forget that law, and they get busted. Hard. Think about it, Mac, an eternity in the original Big House, or a simple 10 percent of take, *rounded up.*

Mr. G

THE LUNATIC (CORNELL UNIVERSITY)

When it was founded in 1894, *The Lunatic,* Cornell's humor magazine, was jauntily called *The Widow.* Editor David

Graham recounts *The Widow* was dedicated to "the legend of the college widow: a flirtatious young woman who played with freshman's affections." Sadly, she (the magazine) died in 1965.

Happily, it was reincarnated in 1978, a more radical beast born under the guidance of The Cornell Liberation Army. It was no *Widow*, taking on a more reckless attitude, parodying children's magazines, the power elite, and sex, drugs and politics.

Classic spoofs from the early years include "Everything You Ever Wanted To Know About Bowling," "Goy's Life," and "Missing Children Trading Cards." Though there have been occasional lapses in publication due to untimely graduations of the editorial staff, *The Lunatic* enjoys a healthy campus output.

The Sexual Prowess Quiz

Are you sex starved? A social misfit? Find out with our portable evaluation. You have ten minutes to complete the test. Do not cheat off your neighbor, though you may cheat on your neighbor. Keep your hands out of your pockets. We know what they're doing in there.

1) When an attractive member of the opposite sex bumps into you, do you:
a) Say "Excuse me," and introduce yourself.
b) Stare lecherously and salivate.
c) Say "Now that we've bumped, how 'bout we grind?"
d) Open up your trench coat.

2) For a first date, do you prefer:

a) A romantic candlelight dinner followed by a moonlight stroll on the beach.

b) *The Rocky Horror Picture Show* followed by mutual heroin abuse in a mosh pit.

c) Going to see *Bambi* with your mom sitting between you and sharing a soda (two straws of course).

d) Going to see a monster truck show with the hillbillies from *Deliverance*.

3) If it looks like s/he might be willing, do you:

a) Stop at the drugstore and discreetly buy protection.

b) Stop at the pet store and buy a choke collar.

c) Stop at the cash machine.

d) Pull out your zippered leather mask.

4) If your roommate walks in on you, do you:

a) Dress quickly and apologize.

b) Start swearing at her in Punjabi and threaten her until she leaves.

c) Tell him he's blocking the video camera.

d) Ask her to join you.

5) If you had a choice, would you rather:

a) Cure AIDS and never get laid.

b) Achieve world peace and never get laid.

c) Feed the poor and never get laid.

d) It doesn't matter, because you don't think you ever will get laid.

Scoring: If you don't know how to score, you flunk the test anyway.

Open Mikers:
Dina Pearlman

rowing up in Teaneck, New Jersey, Dina Pearlman wanted to be Carol Burnett. "Her show was it for me. I loved all her characters, like Eunice and Mrs. Wiggins." But while most kids with aspirations of performing get to try out their stuff on family, Dina didn't have that option, since she was an only child raised by a single parent, her father.

"I was alone, all the time. But with all this time to myself, I was always sort of creating characters. And acting out full dramas in my mind."

Dina's earliest acclaim came as Mae Peterson in *Bye Bye Birdie*. "At thirteen, I was playing a 65-year-old Jewish

Dina Pearlman

woman. In fact, I won an award for best supporting actress for my performance at my theater camp."

Upon graduation from Carnegie-Mellon University in Pittsburgh, Dina moved to the Upper East Side of Manhattan, across the street from a comedy club called The Comic Strip. "And it was all I could do not to go in there, just to see what it was about. But I was petrified, I was too afraid."

Though she couldn't muster up the nerve for standup, Dina was making the audition rounds in New York. "My agent had just informed me that I got turned down for a part in an off-Broadway play and I was really, really, really, really depressed. So I ordered a pizza and when it was delivered, I was about to sit down and eat the whole thing, as was my custom. In fact, that year I gained about twenty-five pounds, just because the rejection was taking an incredible toll on me."

Having a comedy club for a neighbor proved too great a lure for Dina to resist. "I stopped myself from eating the pizza and, even though I had no material, I said 'I'm going to go to an open mike night and just talk for a couple of minutes.'"

The Hollywood part of the story has Dina boarding a bus at 81st Street in Manhattan. "The open mike was on 53rd Street and I wrote my material on the Second Avenue bus. When I got there, I paid the lady three dollars to go on and I had a gin and tonic to get my nerve up and I went onstage and I just imitated the people in my neighborhood: the Puerto Rican checkout girl in my supermarket, my Italian boyfriend. And it was a phenomenal set."

Of course, Dina didn't realize that succeeding her first

time out virtually guaranteed that she would fail her next twenty times onstage. "I couldn't match that first set for months afterwards. It wasn't until I came to understand how bad it could get up there that I started to get stage fright. If you don't know from bombing, you're not afraid to bomb."

Years after that first night out, though, Dina has crafted her act to include a whole gallery of characters. The characters she's created, from a Jewish matron to the Middle Eastern electronics dealer, have made Dina more than a standup comic. Her act recalls the work of people like Whoopi Goldberg and John Leguizamo. It's less a series of bang-bang punch lines and more character studies. Being a woman in the business of comedy, the obvious questions arise. But when Dina is asked if women have a tougher time in the predominantly male business, she answers in no uncertain terms.

"It's a big fat cliché, and the truth of the matter is it's much easier as a woman. There are so few of us that clubs are dying for women. So we have a tremendous advantage over men."

So, it's easier in terms of the work, but what about the personal life of a female standup? "I'm dating somebody now who's very sophisticated. He's a very successful attorney, a real player. And he's dying to come see my act. I'm not going to let him in the room! There's no better way to possibly detract from my sexual appeal.

"A woman is much more vulnerable than a man onstage. If you notice, most women standups tend to dress very nonsexually. You try to dress nice, but by the same token, you don't want your tits hanging out, and there's a reason for that. Let's face it, tits are not funny."

Dina feels her single-parent childhood has informed her experience in standup comedy. "I was much better armed for dealing with an all-male business having grown up with a man. I used to hear a lot of the women comedians telling me what to look out for, but I really felt I could handle whatever they threw at me because I had been raised by a man."

Dina is philosophical about the state of comedy in the nineties. "The eighties were a really weird time. Everybody had a lot of money. People were really into going out and getting drunk and using cocaine. The nineties are a much more serious time."

Las Vegas and Atlantic City remain two locations where Dina would love to perform. "I love Atlantic City. As a kid, my father used to take me, every year after summer camp, when we'd have to get acquainted again. Every night, he'd go down to the casino and gamble. I guess he'd be cruising chicks down there too, I'm not sure. And I'd be upstairs watching TV. It would be nice to get a gig in AC just so I could perform and then come upstairs and watch TV.

"Whenever I feel down about this business, the one thing that does keep me excited is that God gave me this ability to do almost anything, except sing."

Reading Is Fundamental

If you are going to tell people the truth, be funny or they'll kill you.

—Billy Wilder

kay. We've recommended comedy TV shows, movies, CD-ROMs and albums, and that's all well and good . . . if you happen to have electricity. But what if you're Amish and you still want your comedy dose? Don't you deserve a Jerry, Roseanne, or Lenny to amuse you after a grueling day of barn raising? Of course you do! And that's why we compiled this chapter on books. Now, now, don't be frightened, these are comedy books. No lessons or morals or quadratic equations, nothing to fear but a split in your sides. These are fun books! Books that you can leave in the outhouse magazine rack or pack on that horse and buggy trip to Bermuda.

From our usual exhausting seasons of research, combing bookstores and libraries, we have learned that there are many books out there! Thousands! And a lot of them are funny, too! But, alas, time and space limit our choices to only the

---

THE BOOKS YOU'RE LEAST LIKELY TO FIND STUDY GUIDES FOR

Jackie Collins's *Hollywood Wives*

Where's Waldo?

Horny Anal Nurses

The Bridges of Madison County (though you can find a study guide for the audio version)

Comedy Central: The Essential Guide to Comedy

---

sweetest plums. So Eben, Ezekial, and Zachariah, this book's for you!

SEINLANGUAGE
BY JERRY SEINFELD (BANTAM)

Did you ever wonder what it was like to be a wildly successful standup comic, have the number one TV sitcom, and a best-selling book? Here's a way to find out. Record that little jazzy, pop-pop theme music from "Seinfeld," set up a mike and a spotlight in front of a curtain in your home and read *SeinLanguage* aloud.

Well, how did it feel? It helps if you're rolling in dough, but you get the point. *SeinLanguage* is pretty much the standup routine in book form, but since we all seem to like Jerry's act so much, that's not such a bad thing.

SeinLanguage doesn't hit any uncharted territory—it's pretty much what you've come to expect from Seinfeld (jokes about jawbreakers, shower radios, Superman, etc.) but, nevertheless, it's extraordinarily fun to read.

Broken down into chapters like "Freeway of Love," the chapter is then further divided into segments like "The Date" to "The Sex" to "The Relationship" and, ultimately, "The End."

Here's a sample from the segment entitled "The Date":

I've always wanted to invite a woman up to my apartment for a nightcap then just give her one of those little hats that flops to the side. "That's all. I just wanted to give you that. You can go now. If you want to go out next week, I'll give you a short robe that matches."

I think when you first start dating, they ought to give you three "Get Out of Relationship Free" cards so you can go up to the person and say, "Uh, here you go. I'm sorry. I'll grab my tennis racquet. Don't get up. Best of luck. Sorry." Which is fine—unless, of course, the person you're in the relationship with happens to have an "Eight Months of Guilt, Torture, and Pain" card.

There's no shortage of Seinfeld's own brand of observational humor, and *SeinLanguage* reminds us that Jerry is the master. In the section called "Dining Out," he writes,

> Sometimes you go to a nice restaurant, they put the check in a little book. What is this, the story of the bill? "Once upon a time somebody ordered a salad." There's a little gold tassel hanging down. Am I graduating from the restaurant? Should I put this on the rearview mirror of my Camaro?"

SeinLanguage is not Seinfeld's tell-all book—no confessions here, but it's a refreshing laugh-a-page tome, and frankly, who wants anything else?

HOW TO TALK DIRTY AND INFLUENCE PEOPLE (FIRESIDE/
SIMON AND SCHUSTER)
AN AUTOBIOGRAPHY BY LENNY BRUCE

"I dedicate this book to all the followers of Christ and his teachings; particularly to a true Christian—Jimmy Hoffa—because he hired ex-convicts as, I assume, Christ would have." So starts the autobiography of a man who couldn't sneeze without a controversy. Or does it start with the title, a take-off on Dale Carnegie's self-help bestseller, *How To Win Friends and Influence People?* No, it starts with little Leonard Schneider, aka Lenny Bruce, sitting under the kitchen sink listening to his mother and her friend discuss the speed at which Filipinos come, the size of an African-American member and what to rub where to keep your man.

First published in 1963, *How To Talk Dirty and*

Influence People is not a stringing together of bits. It is The Story of The Man in his own words. And he writes as he speaks—in that Brucian jargon, with unblinking honesty.

Bruce's stories are well known. His life of high drama included arrests, narcotics and the overdose that ultimately killed him. Though the book obviously doesn't cover the story of his death, it is not lacking in color.

Brought up in an unorthodox fashion at the height of the Depression, Bruce lived with his eccentric mother on Long Island, sometimes resorting to black-market chicanery. From there he served in the Navy, seeing combat, hoping to be discharged as a transvestite. Eventually he resorted to dressing as a WAVE. He eloquently relates the story of being worked over by four naval psychiatrists at Newport Naval Hospital.

FIRST OFFICER: Lenny, have you ever actively engaged in any homosexual practice?

LENNY: No sir. (An "active" homosexual is one who does the doing, and the "passive" is one who just lies back. In other words, if you were a kid and you were hitchhiking and some faggot came on with you and you let him do whatever his "do" was, he was an "active" homosexual, and you are a "passive" homosexual if you allowed any of this to happen. You'll never see this in an AAA driving manual, but that's the way it is.)

SECOND OFFICER: Do you enjoy the company of women?

LENNY: Yes, sir.

FOURTH OFFICER: Do you enjoy wearing women's clothing?

LENNY: Yes, sir.

ALL FOUR: When is that?

LENNY: When they fit.

(He received an honorable discharge, but sadly, they took away his WAVE's uniform.)

His checkered cross-dressing past did not interfere with his marriage to stripper Honey Harlowe, a beautiful, Ava Gardner look-alike. Though their union was ill-fated, it was not without charm. The gallant Bruce desperately attempted to make enough money to keep Honey off the stage (one attempt involved traveling through Miami Beach in stolen priest garb soliciting money for a leper colony.)

The rest of the book is the first-hand account of his ascendance to stardom accompanied by tales of the drug and obscenity arrests, along with other painful personal battles.

How To Talk Dirty and Influence People is a surprisingly well written, completely absorbing book. And like Bruce, it is also excruciatingly funny.

METROPOLITAN LIFE (PLUME)
BY FRAN LEBOWITZ

If you're unfamiliar with Fran Lebowitz, she could be described as a 1970s New York literati icon. She's still around, but the seventies were her era. She was part of the Studio 54 crowd, hanging with Andy, Calvin and Bianca.

Much of *Metropolitan Life* consists of reprinted magazine

essays that originally appeared in *Interview, Mademoiselle* and British *Vogue.* They cover everything from the evils of plants to the casualties of city life.

Some might say that *Metropolitan Life* is dated. Lebowitz talks about mood rings, the new digital clocks and pocket calculators, disco, and T.A. (transactional analysis—you know, "I'm Okay, You're Okay"). But hey, if dated material is so bad, how come that Shakespeare guy is so popular? Besides, 1974 or 2074, this stuff is funny.

Lebowitz could be called cynical, sarcastic, savvy, city, street, even adjectives that don't begin with an *s* sound. And though she is very New York, her experiences transcend. On a flight to Milan she describes,

> The flight is uneventful, except that the gentleman to my left, a Milanese flour manufacturer wearing a green mohair suit, falls in love with me and I am compelled to spend the last three hours of the trip pretending to be in a coma.

For straight humor pieces, you can't beat "Vocational Guidance for the Truly Ambitious," a rip-roaring take-off on those neat little tests designed to help people find their calling. In "So You Want to Be The Pope," Lebowitz offers these multiple choice questions.

Of the following, my favorite name is . . .
a. Muffy   b. Vito   c. Ira   d. Jim Bob   e. Innocent XIII

My friends call me . . .
a. Stretch   b. Doc   c. Toni   d. Izzy   e. Supreme Pontiff

For dress-up occasions, I prefer . . .
a. something kicky yet elegant   b. anything by Halston   c. evening pajamas   d. a surplice and a miter.

This bit is followed by, "So you want to be an heiress? an absolute political dictator? a social climber? an empress?" All equally riotous.

PARLIAMENT OF WHORES (VINTAGE)
BY P.J. O'ROURKE

As the White House correspondent for *Rolling Stone* magazine, P.J. O'Rourke has earned a reputation as not only a journalist but a humorist. Even if you don't share O'Rourke's conservative/libertarian bent, this book will make you laugh out loud with its on-target swipes at politicians, lobbyists and the ignorance of the voting public.

Along the way, you will learn a lot about how the system really works, which is probably more scary than funny. In the chapter entitled "Would You Kill Your Mother to Pave I-95?" or "The Federal Budget," here's how O'Rourke describes the budget process:

> The final budget compromise (which is a compromise in the sense that being bitten in half by a shark is a

compromise with being swallowed whole) was "hammered out."... The result ... was more than one thousand pages of legislation—a pile of paper ten inches thick, weighing twenty-four pounds and containing ... Here's an interesting point: Nobody knew what it contained. No one, not one single person in the entire United States had read this document.

In the first place, it's impossible to read the federal budget. Richard Darman, the director of the Office of Management and Budget, actually said so in his introduction. ... "It contains almost 190,000 accounts. At the rate of one per minute, eight hours per day, it would take over a year to reflect upon these!"

Hah! Hah! Hah! Er, uh, hmmm. Oh well.

If you want to learn more about P.J. O'Rourke, try *Give War a Chance* (Vintage), which focuses on the international scene. O'Rourke details his adventures in Ulster, Riyadh and other hot spots around the world.

COUPLEHOOD (BANTAM)
BY PAUL REISER

Appearing on "Oprah," Paul Reiser, who was promoting this book, recounted tales of the tens of thousands of couples that approached him on a daily basis proclaiming "We're Jamie and Paul! That's exactly us!" The Jamie and Paul they speak of are the characters Paul Reiser and Helen Hunt play on the hit series "Mad About You." What they mean is that they are like Jamie and Paul Buchman (or they think they are) in that they as a couple also do silly, quirky things that

they take very seriously. Of course, Jamie and Paul are fictitious. They appear for a half hour a week in prime time. And there's only so much material they can cover. Which is where *Couplehood* picks up.

Unlike Paul Buchman, Paul Reiser is a real person, and he has a real wife (named, oddly, Paula. Paul and Paula. Cute). This is their story. Well, not really. *Couplehood is,* however, a humorous, insider's guide to marriage. It's not going to shake up the *Men Are From Mars, Women Are From Venus* school, but it's going to make all those annoying Buchman wannabees even more annoying.

Several of the topics the ex-stand-up comic covers have a familiar resonance: "Chicken or Fish," "I Just Need Two Minutes," and this idea:

> Certain realities of marriage don't kick in right away. I was married six, seven months . . . and then it just hit me . . . I'm never going to be with any other woman naked, ever? Seriously? . . . In other words, out of all the different people, body types, shapes, and sizes, you're saying: These are the last breasts I'm ever gonna touch? Interesting. . . . I don't think I understood that.
> . . . Just to clarify. . . . What you're saying is: These hands will not touch the skin of another woman for, literally, ever? No matter what. . . . Even if we're in

different countries? Or we're mad at each other or something? Uh-huh . . . So, you're saying, basically, "No." . . . "No" would be the word for me to hang on to here . . . Geez. And the same for you? I'm the last guy you're ever going to see naked? Wow . . . well, good luck to you.

Very funny human stuff. Oh, and the book begins on page 145, because Reiser feels it's so overwhelming to start a book and be on only, say page 8. This way you start, and you're already smack in the middle. And it feels like you only just started!

PRIVATE PARTS (SIMON AND SCHUSTER)
BY HOWARD STERN

Like his radio and television shows, Howard Stern's book, *Private Parts* is often brilliantly funny, smart, and sometimes profound. When it's not, it's like a grisly car wreck you can't take your eyes off.

But one thing it is never, and that is boring. We'd smack down twenty-three bucks for that alone.

Beginning with a bang, so to speak, the first chapter involves lesbians *and* masturbation. Warning: There's a lot of that kind of stuff, and nudity, too.

But, there are also copies of scrawled hate mail—"Howard: Your show sucks. . . . Why don't you do plastic surgery on your ugly face . . ."—samples of his strange art work and endless diatribes on celebrities who irritate him (Chevy Chase, Regis and Kathie Lee). There are glimpses behind the scenes at the Stern show, complete with photos of all those bizarre fringe people, and many intimate details of Howard's life (if you listen to his show, you already know how much Howard likes to share).

In one of the most absorbing chapters, "It Was the Worst of Times, It Was the Worst of Times," Stern recounts the story of his life, so far. The first section begins with a picture of baby Howard drooling, entitled "Raised Like a Veal," then goes on to describe his kooky family and finally his first job entertaining as a puppeteer. (He began doing a production of *Fiddler on the Roof* at an old-age home, but quickly degenerated into dirty puppet shows for his friends.)

Private Parts is the kind of book you could pick up at any point and start reading. A great one for the rest room magazine rack.

NAKED BENEATH MY CLOTHES (VIKING PENGUIN)
BY RITA RUDNER

If you don't like Rita Rudner's book *Naked Beneath My Clothes,* you might at least appreciate the flip cartoon of Rita in a cocktail dress swan diving down the side of the pages into a small pool of water.

But most likely, you will enjoy the book. It's a soft-breeze-that-takes-you-by-surprise kind of funny. If the bombastic raunch of *Private Parts* leaves you a little overwhelmed, Rudner can provide sweet relief.

STERN PICKS WHO'S HOT, WHO'S NOT

Chevy Chase—never been funny funny.

Alan King—funny until he did those stupid Toyota commercials.

Jerry Seinfeld—funny.

Elaine Boosler—lame.

Albert Brooks—always funny.

Woody Allen—not funny now. His testimony's a riot, though.

Bob Hope—was one of the greats.

Rudner is one of the top women comics, as well as a budding filmmaker, and the tone of her book is similar to that of her act. You can almost hear her voice in your head as you read some chapter titles: "What Is It With Men And Their Cars?," "Should I Get My Head Analyzed, or Just My Hair?" and "Survival Of The Fattest."

I've belonged to many gyms in my life. I like to take advantage of special offers. "JOIN NOW!! GET LAST YEAR FREE!! . . . PUT NO MONEY DOWN, YOU WON'T COME ANYWAY!!"

I think of all the gym ads I've seen, my favorite was Cher's. I was checking into a hotel once, and there was a life-size cutout of her, beneath which a caption read:

Cher says, "Excuses won't lift your butt."

Rita says, "There has to be a better way to put that." I'm working on it—so far I only have:

Cher says, "If you're going to dance naked onstage in your forties, you're going to have to spend a lot of time at the gym."

There are the user-friendly lists we love so much, such as "Things That Sound Better Than They Are" (being a princess), "Things That Are Better Than They Sound" (V-8 juice), "Things You'll Never Hear Me Say in a Restaurant" (I make this better at home) and "Things I Hope I Never Have To Say in a Restaurant" (I make this better at home).

If that doesn't get you, the adorable cartoons and precious photos will.

IF YOU'RE TALKING TO ME, YOUR CAREER MUST BE IN TROUBLE (HYPERION)
BY JOE QUEENAN

Hollywood is full of phony, two-faced butt-smoochers. Joe Queenan is not one of them. Rather far from it, to be frank. A writer who goes beyond telling it like it is, Queenan pulls off Hollywood's muumuu and exposes its big, cellulite-covered rolls.

With pieces culled from the pages of *Movieline, Rolling Stone,* and other publications, *If You're Talking to Me* packs a hilarious wallop, taking aim at stars from Barbra Streisand (regarding her role in *Nuts* as a $500-a-night call girl, Queenan says that for "a girl answering the physical description of Barbra Streisand, . . . $85-a-night was more in the general price range. Room included.") to Mickey Rourke (he decides to become him for a day, foregoing bathing for a week prior).

In "Oh, You Beautiful Doll or Are Sean Young's Days Numbered," (a piece that certainly fits in with the book's title), Queenan interviews Sean Young in her apartment while she's having her algebra lesson. He is subtle, here, probably because Young is such an easy target. Nevertheless, he does what needs to be done.

> As this weeks algebra lesson breaks up, conversation turns to the subject of Lulov's [her teacher's] name. "It's a Jewish name," he explains. "It's the Hebrew word for palm. Like Palm Sunday."
>
> "I was just confirmed!" Young interjects excitedly. "It's amazing how much the Jewish and Catholic religions are tied in. Jesus was a Jew."
>
> Wasn't he, though? And, truly, there is something endearing in all of this, something elfishly reassuring that in an era where many starlets want to impress strangers with how much they learned in college, Young is willing to reveal how much she didn't learn in high school.

Rarely mild, sometimes quite caustic, Queenan slices and dices the best of the screen idols, presenting a salad of clever criticism served with a sneer and sure to make you howl.

ROY BLOUNT'S BOOK OF SOUTHERN HUMOR (NORTON)
EDITED BY ROY BLOUNT, JR.

"If you only buy one humor book this year, but *Roy Blount's Book of Southern Humor*! You won't be sorry!" (This is not an actual quote, but doesn't it sound like one?) Seriously, at 668 pages, you probably won't need another book of any kind . . . ever.

Self-proclaimed son of the South, Roy Blount, Jr. amassed the exotic potpourri of Southern humor found in *Roy Blount's Book of Southern Humor.* Included in the selections are folk tales, essays, poems, song lyrics, short stories and memoirs by such vastly heterogeneous creators as William Faulkner, Louis Armstrong, Flannery O'Connor, Lyle Lovett, Eudora Welty, Justin Wilson, Zora Neale Hurston, and many, many more.

Blount's witty and charming writing gives the pieces' introductions just the right spin. In "Various Black Virginians as told to Daryl Cumber Dance," he writes,

Shuckin' and Jivin': Folklore from Contemporary Black Americans, published in 1978, derived from fieldwork done for a doctoral dissertation at Virginia Commonwealth University by Daryl Cumber Dance (the only woman named Daryl I have ever heard of aside from Daryl Hannah) . . . gathered stories and verses from black Virginians.

When I Say "Scat"
There was a fellow who had about ten or twelve cats at his house, you know, and he had ten little holes in

his door. One day he had a lot of visitors to come to his house, you know—men friends. And so one of 'em said to 'im, say, "John," say, "why is it that you have so many holes in that door? You got ten cats, but all of 'em can go out one hole, can't they?"

He say, "Yeah, but when I say 'Scat!' I mean scat!"

There is also work from Blount himself, such as his poem, "Song to Oysters."

> I like to eat an uncooked oyster.
> Nothing's slicker, nothing's moister.
> Nothing's easier on your gorge
> Or, when the time comes, to dischorge.
> But not to let it too long rest
> Within your mouth is always best.
> For if your mind dwells on an oyster . . .
> Nothin's slicker, nothing's moister.
>
> I prefer my oyster fried.
> Then I'm sure my oyster's died.

Blount also includes pieces from classic humor novels such as Charles Portis's *Norwood,* and *Confessions from a Failed Southern Lady* by Florence King. A nice way to sample a variety of southern dishes without having to pay a la carte.

TRUE STORY (RANDOM HOUSE)
A COMEDY NOVEL BY BILL MAHER

Knowing Bill Maher as the creator/host of Comedy Central's wildly popular talk show "Politically Incorrect," you may question his abilities as a novelist. Sure, his show's success is due as much to Maher's intelligent, witty, and unabashed style as his colorful panelists. But what does that have to do with fiction? What does a standup comedian know about denouement, engaging protagonists, and tables of contents? Evidently, plenty.

True Story (as in "True story—I'm on a bus to Atlantic City and there's a nun, a rabbi, and a clown . . .") takes place during the early eighties, at the beginning of the comedy boom. Five very different, would-be standup comics, Fat, Chink, Shit, Dick and Buck, are the focus—they eat, sleep, breathe and screw comedy. They exist in the time before cable comedy, post-Lenny Bruce, pre-"Seinfeld." They're often pathetic, sometimes sad, but always funny. There aren't many people who could have written this book. To know this world as well as Maher does, you had to be there.

And the stories in the book are all 100 percent true! Not really, but they're frighteningly close. (The book is dedicated "To my friends in comedy. The good parts are all you.")

Between the poignant, human stuff, you'll enjoy reading the excerpted acts. Warning: it's a little blue.

Men have no penis control. It's a tragedy because we get blamed for stuff we can't help . . . when you're consoling a woman and she's crying, so you're consoling her, and you're hugging her, and you get like a grief on? . . . "Honey, I'm sorry, I couldn't help it, in my head I feel really bad . . . down here, I feel a little better . . . no really I think it's horrible that your mother died, now lemme help you off with your bra."

The stories in *True Story* would make for an interesting book on their own, but Maher's crisp, adept writing makes it a winning piece of literature. TRULY!

DUPLEX PLANET (EVERYBODY'S ASKING WHO I WAS) (FABER AND FABER) BY DAVID GREENBERGER

When David Greenberger got a job as activities director at the Duplex Nursing Home, he had no idea what he'd stumbled into. In fact, his lack of experience in the field caused the home to lower his pay by fifty cents an hour.

The inhabitants of the home were a gold mine. Or at least the things they said. Soon after arriving, Greenberger began questioning the residents and compiling their answers. Pretty soon he had a modest newsletter, "The Duplex Planet," that grew into quite a cult object. The best of "The Planet" is here in this book, loved by everyone but the residents themselves. (They didn't find it very interesting.)

The book is set up with questions and lists of answers, including the names of the interviewee. They are sometimes straight, sometimes boring, sometimes sad, and often ho-ha-hilarious. Here's a sampling.

What would the title of your autobiography be?
"A Champion of America!" Walter Kieran

"Autobiography of Ernest Noyes Brookings" Ernie Bookings

"Round the Corner with Bill" Bill LaGasse

"This would probably be a title: The Life of Someone Named William." Bill Niemi

How close can you get to a penguin?

"Probably about five feet." George Vrooman

Walter Kieran: Grab 'em.

DG: You can get that close?

Walter Kieran: Sure!

DG: Why would you want to grab one?

Walter Kieran: For a souvenir.

If you woke up and were six inches taller, what would be the first thing you'd do?

"I'd take a shower and get some decent clothes." Abe Surgecoff

"I'd see a psychiatrist," Jack Mudurian

"Well, after I got through lookin' in the mirror I'd show myself off." Bill LaGasse

Who is Frankenstein?

"He was a monster. He'd grab everybody in sight." John Fay

"He's a tall bastard." David Brewer

"He's an outstanding man. I watched him on programs and I think he's an outstanding man and he's liked by several people." Francis McElroy

"Jewish ain't he?" Walter Kieran

"He was a good ball player, he played for the Yankees, he used to play center field with Joe DiMaggio and Keller. And he used to hit the ball two thousand miles." Harold Farrington

THE PORTABLE DOROTHY PARKER (VIKING)

Walking around with *The Portable Dorothy Parker* tucked under your arm (front side facing out) is like walking around with a sign on your head that says "I am not only *tres* smart, but *tres* witty, too!" That is not the reason we're recommending this book, but it's a nice bonus.

Dorothy Parker was a tragic and eccentric literary figure from the 1920s to the 1950s. She is well-known not from the cinematic bomb *Mrs. Parker and the Vicious Circle* starring Jennifer Jason Leigh but for the pithy quotations she spouted at The Algonquin Round Table (where she once said, regarding the women of the Yale prom, "If they were laid end to end, I wouldn't be a bit surprised").

The Portable contains not only Mrs. Parker's short fiction and poetry, but also her magazine articles, book and play reviews. You may be surprised, if you're not familiar with her work, just how timely it remains.

In the short fiction, "A Telephone Call," we are privy to a voice inside a head waiting for a man to call that sounds surprisingly like Elaine from "Seinfeld."

> Please, God, let him telephone me now. Dear God, let him call me now. I won't ask anything else of You, truly I won't. It isn't very much to ask. It would be so little of You, God, such a little, little thing. Only let him telephone now. Please, God. Please, please, please . . .

And as far as the poems, these are not stuffy sonnets or pretentious lyricisms. You may sense her somewhat grim

217

view in such classics as "Unfortunate Coincidence" and "Resume."

Once you've finished, look at one of the Dorothy Parker biographies. *What Fresh Hell is This*, by Marion Mead, is a good one to start with. It will give you new insight into the exhaustive, kooky genius who lived it.

KEEP READING	
Woody Allen	*Getting Even*
	Without Feathers
Russell Baker	*So This is Depravity*
Dave Barry	*Dave Barry Talks Back*
	Dave Barry Turns 40
	Dave Barry Slept Here
Robert Benchley	*Of All Things*
Ambrose Bierce	*Devil's Dictionary*
Bill Cosby	*Fatherhood*
Cathy Crimmins	*The Secret World of Men: A Girl's Eye View*
Quentin Crisp	*The Naked Civil Servant*
Carrie Fisher	*Postcards from the Edge*
Cynthia Heimel	*If You Can't Live Without Me, Why Aren't You Dead Yet?*
	Sex Tips for Girls
Molly Ivins	*I Can't Believe She Said That!*
Steve Martin	*Cruel Shoes*
Groucho Marx	*The Groucho Letters*

Jackie Mason	*The World According to Me!*
Monty Python's Flying Circus	*The Meaning of Life*
S.J. Perleman	*Baby, It's Cold Inside*
	The Swiss Family Perleman
James Thurber	*Fables for Our Time & Famous Poems*
	My Life and Hard Times
Mark Twain	*The Innocents Abroad*
	The Gilded Age

OPEN MIKERS:
TOM RHODES

Tom Rhodes looks more like he should be playing bass for The Red Hot Chili Peppers than doing standup comedy.

The 28-year-old, long haired comic from Florida, ("that's where I'm from because that's where I learned to drive and lost my virginity"), professes to a rock-and-roll image that his audience perceives as well. "People think I'm Led Zeppelin on the road," admits Rhodes.

It wasn't always that way. Rhodes, who started doing comedy at age seventeen remembers, "My father drove me to my first open mike night, and I was embarrassed, so I made him wait in the car."

It's hard to imagine Rhodes starting out. He is one of those comics who seems like he was born with a mike in his hand. He has a unique style and is, of course, extremely funny, but what distinguishes him is an innate sense of standup. He never loses his cool or gets flustered. Stand up is his track, and he's the Metroliner of comedy. "It's a divine calling," he affirms.

Not given to straight answers, he'll tell you he got into comedy because, "I killed a man, it's my community service." And he gets his material from "three midgets in Ohio."

But seriously folks. Rhodes gets his real comic stimulus from life. "It's funny when someone steps in dog shit or hits their knee on the coffee table."

Rhodes is quick to deflect the notion of doing standup to get to a sitcom, although NBC decided to give him one anyway. "I call TV the devil box," Rhodes declares. "I never had any desire to be on TV. I did stuff for Comedy Central, and that's gravy, man." The "stuff" for Comedy Central are MTV-esque promos, with Rhodes in a variety of settings doing his bits. In one, he appears in an abandoned building, very in-your-face. "I like rap music, I just don't like when they're a little too 'down with whitey.' You know, I buy a rap album and I'm like wow, these guys are great, I can really get into this, then they start going 'Kill honky, whitey . . . ' And I'm like WHOOOOA! Hey! That's me, man! I'm the one who bought the cassette, I paid $10.99! . . . I love seeing white suburban kids trying to pull off the whole gangster attitude. You see 'em at the mall, 'They just don't feel the vibe I'm putting out at the yogurt shop . . . Yo bitch! I didn't ask for no sprinkles! What up!' Sorry D.J. Jazzy Trevor, I didn't know the food court was yours, buddy."

Rhodes is philosophical about what he sees as the waning of comedy clubs. "There used to be too many standups, now there aren't enough." It's not all bad, though, "All those strip mall suburban clubs have gone out of business, and so has the strip-mall comedian." Rhodes likes the new direction comedy seems to be taking. "It's gone back to the cities where it belongs," he muses happily. "You'll see a comic, hear some music, see a comic, hear some music." He adds "I think it's going to return to being a jazz thing again, like when Lenny Bruce was doing it. And that," he declares, "is the ultimate."

Turn Out
the Lights . . .
Dave's Coming On

All my humor is based on destruction and despair. If the whole world was tranquil, without disease and violence, I'd be standing in the bread line.

—Lenny Bruce

Is there something in the American psyche that requires us to laugh before going to bed? Is it written somewhere that sleep cannot be attained without first sitting through a monologue or a sketch? If you were to ask a group of television programmers those questions, you can bet that the answer would be a resounding "yes."

Comedy at bedtime has been a staple since the beginning of television. In fact, before the advent of TV, comedians would go door-to-door between 11 and 12 o'clock every night, visiting people's homes and doing monologues to put them to sleep. But that was before Carson, Leno, O'Brien, Letterman, Snyder, and that Australian infomercial guy with the vegetable slicer.

In this chapter, we'll look at the curious phenomenon of late night comedy. So prop up the pillow, slip between the sheets and turn off the TV, for God's sake! Will it kill you to do a little reading for once?

THE LEAST-REMEMBERED LATE NIGHT TALK SHOWS

"Thicke of the Night"

"The Wilton North Report"

"Into the Night Starring Rick Dees"

"The Pat Sajak Show"

"Nightlife Starring David Brenner"

"The Whoopi Goldberg Show"

"The Last Word"

In 1950, NBC premiered "Broadway Open House." A precursor to "The Tonight Show," "Broadway Open House" was the first late night comedy show. Hosted by comedian Jerry Lester and featuring Morey Amsterdam, "Broadway Open House" was comprised of sketches, music and interview segments.

Low ratings ended "Broadway Open House" after only fourteen months, but the show proved that there was an audience for late night comedy. In 1954, NBC gave a young comic and songwriter named Steve Allen the chance to host "The Tonight Show."

"The Tonight Show," under Steve Allen, was ninety live minutes of music, interviews and comedy. Allen, like Ernie Kovacs, was one of the first broadcasters to understand the power of television and he used it to its full extent. The camera was an extension of his imagination, leading him out to the streets of Manhattan or into the depths of the Hudson Theater, where his show was produced.

Coincidentally, when Steve Allen left "The Tonight Show" in 1957 to do a prime-time show for NBC, Ernie Kovacs took over as host of the late night show for about four months. In part, his tenure was short because Kovacs did comedy exclusively for the home audience. His material involved camera tricks and special effects that the audience in the Hudson Theater could not see. They were left staring at the studio monitors—in effect, expecting theater but left to watch television. Kovacs almost never used a studio audience on any of his subsequent television shows.

The post-Kovacs "Tonight Show" was hosted by Jack Paar, and it moved a little closer to what the show would eventually become. Paar's interviews were supplemented by periodic visits from a variety of regulars, including Dody Goodman, Pat Harrington, Jr. and Cliff Arquette. (Trivia alert: He was also Charlie Weaver on the original "Hollywood Squares" and the paternal grandfather of Rosanna, Patricia, David and Alexis Arquette.)

Throughout his tenure as the host of "Tonight," Paar became well-known for his tantrums and snits. More than once, he claimed he would quit. He once walked off the show because NBC cut a joke he told which included the term *water closet* (which, for our readers under 90-years-old, is a colloquialism for *bathroom*).

In 1962, when Paar finally did quit, NBC hired Johnny Carson, a young comic and game show host, to take over the job. Carson's easygoing, personable style made him a natural to ease America to sleep. His cool detachment was a welcome change from the emotional bluster of his pre-

STUFF YOU MIGHT NOT KNOW ABOUT "THE TONIGHT SHOW"

- Johnny Carson's only film appearance: opposite Connie Francis in *Lookin' for Love.*

- The composer of the Carson "Tonight" theme: Mr. "My Way" himself, Paul Anka.

- The composer of the Leno-era "Tonight" theme: Branford Marsalis.

- Among the writers on the Paar-era "Tonight:" Dick Cavett, David Lloyd ("The Mary Tyler Moore Show"), Marshall Brickman *(Annie Hall).*

- In addition to being an oft-married talk show host, Johnny Carson can list "magician," "drummer" and "Academy Awards host" on his resume.

- Carson once devoted an entire ninety-minute "Tonight" to Jim Garrison, the New Orleans D.A. who investigated the Kennedy assassination.

- Carson-era "Tonight" producer Fred DeCordova directed the classic *Bedtime for Bonzo.*

- Carson and Letterman once employed Judge Wapner to settle a dispute about Letterman's pickup truck, which Carson considered an eyesore in their Malibu neighborhood.

- Carson invited Steven Wright back to "The Tonight Show" only two weeks after the comic's debut appearance.

- Comic Bobby Kelton is the only standup comic to have generated a spontaneous standing ovation on Carson's "Tonight."

- Dana Carvey was once considered as Leno's "Tonight" sidekick.

decessor. If he didn't have the antic energy of an Allen or a Kovacs, he also wasn't awash in bathos, like Jack Paar.

As Carson's power grew at NBC, he was able to dictate the future of "The Tonight Show." His production company assumed partial ownership of the show in the early seventies, giving Carson a piece of the lucrative syndication profits. As part of his contract negotiations in the early eighties (when he was said to be responsible for 17 percent of NBC's pretax profits), he got "The Tonight Show" cut from ninety to sixty minutes. His work week was eventually reduced from five nights to four, with Mondays devoted to "The Best of Carson," which turned out to be a great way to watch Brenda Vaccaro plugging a two-year-old movie. (Carson's schedule was later reduced even further from four nights to three: reruns on Mondays and guest hosts on Tuesdays.) He dictated who would guest host during his twelve weeks of vacation. And his production company was given the time slot following the show to develop a series.

When compared with the comedy of people like Steve Allen and Ernie Kovacs, Carson's "Tonight" bits were tame and unimaginative. His "Floyd R. Turbo, American" bits were flabbily written diatribes for a John Bircher who looked like Elmer Fudd. "Art Fern and the Tea Time Movies" was an excuse for Carson to play an oily afternoon-movie host and leer at the Matinee Girl played by Carol Wayne. (Tawdry Trivia Alert: A regular on the seventies game show "Celebrity Sweepstakes," Wayne appeared in a pictorial in a 1984 issue of *Playboy*. She later drowned mysteriously in Mexico.) A typical cast and title for one of Art's blockbusters was Cesar Romero, Desi Arnaz, Pedro Armendariz, Gilbert Roland and Hayley Mills in "Gidget Goes to Spanish Harlem."

Though Carson's sketch material was weak, it was acknowledged that he was the master of the monologue. His timing and delivery were sharp enough to overcome the most hackneyed material. Indeed, some of his biggest laughs came from his "savers," the takes or lines he'd use to rescue himself from a joke that bombed.

The comedy that really hit on Carson's "Tonight" was the unplanned stuff, the bits that just took off on their own. Whether it was the famous clip of Ed Ames and Johnny landing a tomahawk in the groin of a wooden Indian ("Welcome to 'Frontier Bris' ") or a loopy Doc Severinsen recounting to Carson how Thanksgiving played a large part in the bandleader's most recent divorce ("I wanted oyster stuffing with the turkey and she wanted bread stuffing, and she got bread stuffing and a *lot* of money!"), spontaneity was the source of some of Carson's most memorable moments.

When Carson announced his retirement in 1992, the drama of choosing a new host played itself out in front of millions of people. As Bill Carter reported in his entertaining and exhaustively researched book, *The Late Show,* the job of finding someone to front one of the most successful television franchises in history wasn't just a matter of choosing a good haircut and a pleasing baritone to lull America to sleep. Rather, it became a matter of national importance, ending with Carson protégé David Letterman being wooed by the other three networks while his most frequent guest, Jay Leno, was awarded the host's chair.

Leno's stint as host of the show has not been problem-free: his longtime manager, Helen Kushnick, was fired from the show's executive producer position after alienating staff members and network executives. She subsequently died of cancer. Bandleader Branford Marsalis left the show in early 1995. And for the first time since Johnny Carson was host, "The Tonight Show" is not alone at the front of the late night ratings pack. It shares that honor with the man NBC dismissed, David Letterman, and his "Late Show" on CBS.

Nice segue, huh?

David Letterman came to NBC in the late seventies with a highly-regarded, yet short-lived morning talk show. In effect, the show was what would become "Late Night with David Letterman," the series that Johnny Carson's company produced when Carson negotiated control of the 12:30 time slot with NBC. (Letterman got the same deal with CBS in 1993, resulting in his company, Worldwide Pants, producing "The Late Late Show with Tom Snyder.") A mix of taped comedy pieces and live guests, the show was killed by low ratings after three months but later won a daytime Emmy.

Letterman sat around under contract to NBC until February 1982, when "Late Night" premiered. It took a while for Letterman to hit his stride as an interviewer; that is, he not only had to learn how to listen, he also had to master the difference between a ready quip and a withering barb. Too many of his early guests expecting the former were stung by the latter.

From the beginning, though, "Late Night" was truly original. Rare was the night when there wasn't a camera down on the streets around Rockefeller Center, whether it was to ask passersby for a look at their just-developed photos or to show a huge klieg light projecting hand shadows on the office building across Sixth Avenue.

Letterman encouraged a randy, frat-boy atmosphere on "Late Night." During one show, the cast and crew of NBC's "Today Show" were taping a prime-time special six floors below the "Late Night" studios in Rockefeller Center. Letterman disrupted the taping by bellowing out an office window with a bullhorn. His shenanigans caused a rift with Bryant Gumbel that lasted for more than a year.

As he has continued to do on "Late Show," Letterman made stars of the people in the neighborhood, most notably book editor Meg Parsont. Parsont's office was directly across the street from an office adjacent to the "Late Night" studios. Beginning in early 1990, Letterman visited, via telephone and TV camera, with Parsont in her office. The camera would shoot out one of NBC's office windows into Parsont's and Dave Letterman would talk with her on the phone. His visits graduated from simple discussions of how

STUFF YOU MIGHT NOT KNOW ABOUT LETTERMAN

- Letterman's first regular TV gig was on a summer replacement series starring The Starland Vocal Band.

- The first guest on the last "Late Night" was Tom Hanks, who was also the opening night guest on "Late Show."

- When a guest dropped out, the producers of "Late Night" always called Tony Randall to fill in.

- Until they sang "I Got You Babe" on "Late Night," Sonny and Cher had not performed together publicly in over ten years.

- In its eleven-year run, "Late Night" traveled to Chicago, Las Vegas and Los Angeles and broadcast an entire ninety-minute episode from a plane bound for the Bahamas.

- Among the catch phrases "Late Night" foisted on an unsuspecting public: "What do you want for nothing, wicker?" "I do and I do and I do for you kids and this is the thanks I get!"

- Among the characters played by Chris Elliott on "Late Night:" The Panicky Guy, The Regulator Guy, The Guy Under the Seats, Marlon Brando, Marv Albert, Chris Elliott, Jr.

- Letterman's only movie role: a grizzled old salt in Chris Elliott's *Cabin Boy.*

- This is not to say that Letterman hasn't tried out for other roles. In fact, a tape, shown once on "Late Night," has Dave auditioning for the part that Robert Hays played in *Airplane.*

- Dave's second regular TV gig: working alongside Michael Keaton and Swoosie Kurtz as a member of the troupe on Mary Tyler Moore's late-seventies variety show.

TOP TEN CATEGORIES OF TOP TEN LATE NIGHT WITH DAVID LETTERMAN LISTS

Top Ten Words That Almost Rhyme with Peas

Top Ten Canine Disorders or Debutant Complaints

Top Ten Ways Life Would Be Different If Dogs Ran the World

Top Ten Signs That Your Wife Is Seeing Sinatra

John Gotti's Top Ten Tax Tips

Top Ten Fun Things About Being Mikhail Gorbachev

Top Ten Other Inventions by the Suicide Machine Doctor

Top Ten Ways the World Would Be Different If Everyone Were Named Phil

Jim Bakker's Top Ten Pickup Lines

Top Ten Numbers Between One and Ten

Parsont spent her weekend to elaborate productions in which Jerry Vale appeared at Parsont's office to sing, or she would be asked to drop beach balls out her window to a stage manager below holding a laundry basket on 50th Street.

These out-of-the-studio antics have resulted in comparisons of Letterman to Steve Allen. Even some of Letterman's studio pranks have echoed Allen's, like dunking himself in a big vat of substances. In the fifties, Allen found himself swimming around in a huge tub of gelatin. In the eighties, Letterman took the concept one step further and donned a jumpsuit covered with Alka-Seltzer tablets. He was then lowered into a tank of water to create the biggest antacid ever. Another evening, a 100-gallon tank of dip was rolled out so that Dave, in a suit covered with tortilla chips, could be lowered into the dip and then walk into the audience so they could "snack like crazy."

In 1993, the late night landscape changed, as Letterman jumped from NBC to CBS to assume hosting duties an hour earlier on "Late Show with David Letterman."

Letterman's "Late Show" differs from "Late Night" primarily in scope and size. An 11:30 p.m. audience expects a bigger, livelier show while the pace can be funkier and more relaxed for the 12:30 crowd. The band is bigger now, the stage more expansive and the show is produced at street level in the Ed Sullivan Theater, so when there's something to be done in the neighborhood, Dave can just walk out and take part, whether it's shooting baskets with the Knicks or going to the tux shop next door with Rosie Perez. In Rockefeller Center, he was forced to use emissaries from the audience, or Larry "Bud" Melman, because he couldn't stop the show to take the elevator down to the street.

"Late Show" has given CBS its first chance to compete in late night since its premiere in August 1993. At the time of this writing, however, Leno's "Tonight Show" is beating "Late Show" in the ratings.

And what about "Tonight?" Critics were almost universally harsh on Leno at the beginning, faulting both his stilted delivery and hackneyed material. Many took personally the fact that Leno made no reference to Johnny Carson on the night of his debut. With the departure of Helen Kushnick, Leno began to take a more active role in the production of "Tonight," implementing small but significant changes in the set and placement of the band. Those changes, along with an emphasis on more sketches and taped comedy pieces, have helped "The Tonight Show" evolve into a professional, if uninspired, hour of television.

"The Tonight Show," in fact, has begun to resemble "The Sammy Maudlin Show," an unctuous talk show filled with show business phonies that originated on "SCTV," which followed "The Tonight Show" for eighteen months in the early eighties, following a successful syndicated run.

"SCTV" was a fictional television network located in the fictional burg of Melonville. It was populated by an assortment of the strangest people ever awarded a broadcasting license. Its president was Guy Caballero, a fedora-wearing fraud who rode a wheelchair despite the fact that his legs were fine, Edith Prickley, the station manager partial to leopard skin, and Johnny LaRue, a chain-smoking booze-hound who produced everything from his own cooking show to a sequel to *Chinatown.*

What made "SCTV" so compelling was its format: instead of simply creating parodies of television programming, the producers and writers of the series created Melonville, an environment in which those parodies could live. This alternate reality added a layer of comedy that informed every sketch and gave "SCTV" post-modern elements that had never been seen in sketch comedy. The city itself was a character, in fact. On "SCTV's" special election coverage, one of the issues on the ballot was whether Esperanto should be adopted as the official language of Melonville.

Within the loopy logic of Melonville, a comic like Sammy Maudlin could go from hosting his own talk show to appearing in *Maudlin's 11,* an "SCTV" movie of the week about a heist in Danny Thomas's dressing room. Bobby

STUFF YOU MIGHT NOT KNOW ABOUT "SCTV"

- Among the films directed by "SCTV" alumni: *Caddyshack* (Harold Ramis), *Once upon a Crime* (Eugene Levy), *Hostage for a Day* (John Candy), *The Experts* (Dave Thomas).

- The only movie featuring any "SCTV" characters: *Strange Brew,* with Dave Thomas and Rick Moranis as the beer-and-donut-obsessed MacKenzie Brothers. They were also the only characters to have their own album, off of which came a hit single ("Take Off"), featuring Geddy Lee from Rush.

- Martin Short's Ed Grimley character came from a bit he used to do naked around his house to amuse his wife.

- Before appearing on "SCTV," Martin Short worked as a sitcom actor in two series: "The Associates," about a Wall Street law firm; and "I'm a Big Girl Now," with Danny Thomas and Diana Canova.

- "SCTV" regulars who went on to appear on "Saturday Night Live": Martin Short, Robin Duke, Tony Rosato. Catherine O'Hara was to become a regular in 1981 but quit before her first appearance.

- Andrea Martin, who created such characters as Edith Prickley and Perini Scleroso, won a Tony Award for her part in the short-lived Broadway musical version of *My Favorite Year.*

- John Candy backed out of hosting the Juno Awards, Canada's version of the Oscars, because ad copy described him as "The Biggest Star in Canada," which he felt was a nasty comment about his weight.

- "SCTV" cast members who have hosted "Saturday Night Live": John Candy, Dave Thomas and Rick Moranis, Catherine O'Hara, Martin Short (with Steve Martin and Chevy Chase). Candy and Eugene Levy were to have hosted the show in 1985, but a brief writers' strike caused the cancellation of that episode.

- John Candy made five movies for John Hughes's company: *Planes, Trains and Automobiles, Uncle Buck, The Great Outdoors, Home Alone,* and *Only the Lonely.*

241

Bittman, a low-rent nightclub comic with a truckload of jewelry and a bad catch phrase ("How are ya?"), could don clown makeup to play Terry Malloy in *On the Waterfront, Again.* And two Canuck brothers could fill airtime chatting about everything from donut shops to stuffing mice in beer bottles in an effort to get the brewery to send a free case.

"SCTV" was an outgrowth of the Canadian branch of Chicago's Second City comedy troupe. The show made stars of John Candy, Catherine O'Hara, Rick Moranis, Martin Short, Harold Ramis and Andrea Martin. The fact that the series didn't originate in Los Angeles or New York meant that the comedy wasn't produced by media savvy producers from the two biggest markets in the country. It gave the comedy a slant that had not been seen before on American television. And it began to make audiences aware of the comedy acumen of a country that had only been known for beer and hockey players.

Canada's latest addition to late night comedy has been The Kids in the Hall, five guys from Toronto whose comedy is based on original and offbeat concepts, with nary a parody in the bunch. Dave Foley, Bruce McCulloch, Kevin McDonald, Mark McKinney and Scott Thompson took the name for their troupe from the old Jack Benny radio show. Benny would often read jokes supplied to him by "the kids in the hall." They were first seen in the United States on HBO and Comedy Central, but the last season of their series followed "Late Show" on CBS. Even when the Kids didn't air in late night, their show always conveyed the attitude that these guys shouldn't be on TV before midnight.

The concepts for their sketches could be deceptively simple: a couple attempting to come up with a clever answering machine message. Or they could be subversive and bizarre: a boy, forbidden to bring home strays does just that, but rather than an abandoned dog or an alley cat, the boy has adopted a businessman who "answers to 'Mr. Stevenson' "; two French-Canadian trappers canoe their way through an office, clubbing the male workers for their suits then offering them to a local haberdasher appreciative of a "fresh kill." Whatever the idea, the execution was always precise, exacting and always to the left of what could be expected in lesser comics.

Subtlety and understatement went a long way toward making The Kids in the Hall even funnier. While the Monty Python guys performed as women, they would do so broadly, as a burlesque. The Kids in the Hall created female characters, often going so far as to shave their bodies. They inhabited the characters they played, and that made their sketch comedy richer and more textured than any that had preceded them.

And among those that had preceded the Kids was, of course, "Saturday Night Live."

"Saturday Night Live" began as a hardly-watched late night comedy show in October 1975. With George Carlin as host and guests Andy Kaufman and Janis Ian, the show was a collection of live sketches and filmed commercial parodies. (Trivia alert: One guest bumped from the premiere telecast was Billy Crystal, who would go on to be an "SNL" regular in 1984 and 1985.)

In the time since its premiere, though, the show's title has become part of the lexicon. It has spawned, for better or worse, an entire video library of films featuring characters who began in sketches on "SNL." In its 20+-year existence, it has gone from being unwatched to must-watched to, at times, unwatchable.

In the beginning, the show was considered both innovative and a bit of a throwback, because as edgy and contemporary as the humor was, the idea of a live, ninety-minute comedy show went back as far as "Your Show of Shows" in the 1950s. The comedy was smart and smartass, created by a group of college-educated, media-savvy 25-year-olds. Anything within their frame of reference was ripe for comedy, from politics to drugs to television to rock and roll.

As "Saturday Night Live" progressed, from cast to cast and producer to producer, the name remained the same, but the show has changed. It has come to represent something larger than it did in its beginning. What began as a loose, free-form comedy show is now viewed as a franchise, a springboard for movie stardom. Chevy Chase was the first of the cast to make the break for the big screen. Three years later, John Belushi and Dan Aykroyd followed suit to make "The Blues Brothers." In the ensuing years, Bill Murray, Eddie Murphy, Billy Crystal, Martin Short, Dana Carvey and Mike Myers all answered the call of Hollywood, with varying degrees of success.

One of the results of the show being used as a breeding ground for movie actors is that the edge that existed in its early days has dulled over time. Though many writers and performers consider the show big-time professional comedy, some of the staff at "Saturday Night Live" view the show as little more than a way station on the road to prime time or the big screen.

In addition, the simplicity that permeated "Saturday

STUFF YOU MIGHT NOT KNOW ABOUT "SATURDAY NIGHT LIVE"

- Two episodes of "SNL" have been broadcast on a seven-second delay. The hosts: Richard Pryor and Andrew "Dice" Clay.

- Producer Lorne Michaels has forbidden one episode of "SNL" hosted by Mr. Television, Milton Berle, from ever being shown again.

- John Belushi's last appearance on "Saturday Night Live" was about five months before his death. He stepped out of a men's room stall in the 1981 Halloween episode, hosted by Donald Pleasance. The band on the show that evening, Fear, was brought to the producers by Belushi.

- That same evening, Fear's performance was cut short by the producers as the band slam-danced with audience members and used profanity over open mikes.

- Harry Shearer was the only cast member to do two stints on "SNL"; one in 1980 and one in 1984. Both times he left as a result of conflicts with the producers.

- The oldest host of "SNL"? Miskel Spillman, an eighty-something grandmother who won the "Anyone Can Host" contest in the late seventies.

- The youngest host? Drew Barrymore in 1982, when she was 7-years-old.

- Charles Rocket was fired after a 1981 show hosted by Charlene Tilton for saying the word *fuck* on the air.

- Among the least-remembered musical guests on "SNL": Dexy's Midnight Runners, Color Me Badd, Esther Satterfield, The Bus Boys.

- The first cast member to host the show: Eddie Murphy when he was still a regular after Nick Nolte dropped out.

Night Live" in its first five years has slowly disappeared. Dan Aykroyd, for example, portrayed Jimmy Carter without the benefit of makeup and prosthetics, choosing only to whiten his hair slightly. In the period since "Saturday Night Live" premiered, however, audiences have sought more realism in their comedy. Hence, "Saturday Night Live" has become a festival of wigs, makeup and facial appliances.

In fact, "Saturday Night Live," simply by virtue of the length of time it has aired, and the turnover in its personnel, has gone from being a groundbreaking, unpredictable ninety minutes of television to a weekly trudge through an hour and a half of one-joke concepts, jokeless sketches and characters who do nothing but spew tired catch phrases. If you can't count on "Saturday Night Live" for laughs anymore, is there any hope left for late night comedy?

There might be. Troupes like Mad TV and The State represent the future of sketch comedy. The writers for Conan O'Brien and his meta-sidekick Andy Richter keep coming up with offbeat, unusual concepts that screw with the concept of late night talk shows.

So, there seems to be a future for late night comedy. And as networks proliferate and more and more programming animals need to be fed, the hope is that post-late-news laughs become the cud on which they can chew.

OPEN MIKERS:
DAVE CHAPPELLE

ave Chappelle was working as a standup comic at age fourteen. At an age when most kids are thinking about acne and dates and finals, Chappelle was walking onto nightclub stages behind comics twice his age. "I couldn't get into the clubs unless I brought my mother with me," Dave remembers. "She'd bring me to open mike nights after school." Of course, there were advantages to having Mom along. If a club owner tried to stiff Dave, "I'd just tell my mother."

In the beginning, Chappelle says, "I would just go onstage and talk about what I did that day. I didn't even know comedians had jokes. And then, I started watching the other comedians and think, 'Hey, man, he said the same shit last week.' Then, I would get up there and say something and remember it. Then I'd say it again and elaborate on it a little bit more. It was all trial and error." Thus was created Dave Chappelle's act.

And his act is what separates Dave from a lot of other comics. In fact, with his combination of observation and irony, Chappelle's material bears more than a passing resemblance to that of Richard Pryor, a performer Chappelle has always considered an idol. "He's the one, man."

At the seasoned age of seventeen, Dave came to New York and got his first TV gig. "The first TV show I did was 'Evening at the Improv.' From there, it just went on and on: 'Caroline's Comedy Hour,' 'MTV Half-Hour Comedy Hour.' " Then the floodgates opened. "You do one of those shows, you can start doing all of them. The year after my first TV shot, I think I did about thirteen television shows."

Ask Dave about his most memorable sets and you'll find that they each occurred on one of those television shows. " 'Comic Relief VI' and my first 'Arsenio Hall Show' were the best for me. The 'Arsenio' was a mark that I had set for myself. In my mind, I was able to say, 'Hey, I'm making it.' On 'Comic Relief,' I had a good set and it was a good set on a show filled with a lot of great comedians."

Dave says David Letterman's show was "the hardest TV show I've ever done. First of all, it's cold out there, literally. Second, I was performing in a suit. I'm not funny in a suit. Every time I wear one, I have flashbacks to being in church with my mother. She'd be yelling at me, 'Get off the floor in your good clothes!' "

Working on television forced Dave to create a stack of

new material. "The first two months after I got to New York, I wrote about a whole new half hour. My first thirty minutes of material had been developed over little chunks of fifteen minutes a week onstage. When I got to New York and stage time became so available, I saw that everyone else's material was more polished, and it made me work harder."

And that he has. Between his standup gigs, Dave has worked as an actor in such films as *Undercover Blues* and *Robin Hood: Men in Tights.* "I was doing standup and somebody said, 'Dave, you want to do a movie?' And I said, 'Ok.' Movies fascinate me. Just being on the set and seeing how they do them." And working with Mel Brooks, the director of *Men in Tights?* "The best," says Dave. "That's like a comedian's dream. It was really cool because Carl Reiner was working on the same lot, shooting *Fatal Instinct.* Watching Mel and Carl hanging out between takes. That was *really* cool."

Despite working both standup and film, Dave would never claim to have some kind of overall career path charted. "I had sort of a vague plan, but I think I just want to be famous enough so that I can always do comedy."

Whether or not he stays in the business, Dave has an unusual aspiration for a guy who's worked as a comic for seven years: he wants to go back to school. "Just to study. I went to one of those arts high schools, like in *Fame.* I didn't take my SATs or any of that. So I might go back to college one day."

Dave Chappelle: look for him. You might see him in movies like *The Nutty Professor* or in his television series, "Buddies." Or he might be that guy in the back row of the lecture hall cracking wise during Intro to Physics.

As standup comedy becomes ubiquitous, the true stand-out standups are fewer and farther between. However, there are a number of other not-quite-star comics who are definitely worth watching.

MARC MARON

First seen widely at Comedy Central, Maron's onstage persona is that of the clever, literate, unnervingly paranoid observer. Maron finds conspiracy, or irony, in everything from smoking sections to homeless food thieves.

Maron Sample

"I don't care what religion you are: Jewish, Catholic, Hindu, Bahai, it's all one big corporation. You know when someone says 'they?' 'They say it's going to rain tomorrow. They control the media.' Well, I'm not paranoid, but there is a 'they,' and they meet once a year on the sixtieth floor of this building. At least, that's what they say. So, I'm going to sit here and wait for them, 'cause I have some questions."

MITCH FATEL

If the shy, quirky, no-luck-with-girls type in the back of the classroom were to become a standup, he'd be Mitch Fatel. Fatel uses his experience as a struggling comic in New York City to elicit true laughs, less from his material and more from his halting, "it's all true" delivery.

Fatel Sample
"They say New Yorkers aren't compassionate people, but I disagree. I was on line waiting to give blood and there were over a hundred people there. 'Course, they had to throw out the guy ahead of me, 'cause he didn't realize it had to be your own blood."

DANA GOULD

Dana Gould is a comic who could be considered more of a performance artist than a standup. Whether he's detailing his drunken mother's holiday rantings or talking about his recovery from a nervous breakdown, there's something about Gould's style that keeps his audiences on guard. There's just enough truth in his style of performing that listeners are never quite sure they're hearing a bit, or something that actually occurred in Gould's life. In the way he keeps crowds unsure and uneasy, Dana can most readily be compared with Andy Kaufman, who went so far as to stage fist fights with cohorts planted in the crowd. Gould has a similar knack for forcing his audience to listen, really listen, to what he has to say.

Gould Sample
There isn't one. His material and performance style are so singular that putting them down on paper doesn't do them justice.

THE FUTURE OF COMEDY

If you are not allowed to laugh in heaven, I don't want to go there.

—Martin Luther

omedy's past and present undoubtedly will have an influence on comedy's future. With the twenty-first century fast approaching, it's reasonable to think that comedy will have a significant place on the Information Superhighway. But just how significant? If this highway lives up to its hype, there will be outlets for every kind of media imaginable.

If you've ever taken a communications course, or talked with someone who has, or read an article about the future of television, or seen *Annie Hall,* then you know who Marshall McLuhan is. In the early sixties, McLuhan referred to the "global village" that mass media would create. As the Superhighway slowly undergoes construction, it's clear that the global village is becoming a reality. The combination of satellite technology and computers has brought the entire world closer together.

As a result, the demand for product becomes greater and

greater every day. And the demand for comedy, as popular as it is, has risen even more. We met with a number of media consulting firms and they told us what they think the surest comedy bets are for the cable dial in the near future.

THE SET UP CHANNEL

Twenty-four hours a day of nothing but set-up lines. Turn to it any time you want to hear "Hey, where you from?" or "What is it with these commercials these days?" Every Sunday evening, there's an hour of classic setups from comics like Bob Newhart ("What if Abe Lincoln had a PR man?") and George Carlin ("There are 200,000 words in the English language, and there are seven of them that you can't say on television.").

JOEYVISION

Very simply: Joey Bishop around the clock. Everything Joey's ever done, from his early TV work, his movies with the Rat Pack, and every one of his talk show appearances. And every Wednesday evening, Joey hosts a screening of his crowning achievement: his appearance as the ghost of Alan Alda's father in *Betsy's Wedding*. JOEYVISION is the Magic of Joey.

THE BLACK AND WHITE CHANNEL

A channel devoted to lovers of black-and-white television, but with a twist. The programs on the channel were originally broadcast in color. But to give them an air of antiquity,

WHEN BAD MOVIES HAPPEN TO GOOD COMEDIANS

1. *After the Fox* (1966)—Peter Sellers plays an Italian movie director. Pee-yew!

2. *Blind Date* (1987)—Bruce Willis, John Laroquette and Phil Hartman star in this tasteless slapstick comedy.

3. *Can I Do It 'Til I Need Glasses?* (1980)—Robin Williams, what were you thinking?

4. *Copacabana* (1947)—Even Groucho Marx can't save this lame comedy.

5. *First Family* (1980)—The great cast, which included Bob Newhart, Gilda Radner, Madeline Kahn, Harvey Korman and Rip Torn couldn't work around an awful script.

6. *Haunted Honymoon* (1986)—Gene Wilder, Gilda Radner and Dom Deluise in a lame chiller spoof.

7. *Ishtar* (1987)—Dustin Hoffman, Warren Beatty, Charles Grodin and Carol Kane in this monument to bad movies.

8. *Johnny Dangerously* (1984)—Michael Keaton and Joe Piscopo play rival crime lords.

9. *1941* (1979)—How could you go wrong with John Belushi and Dan Aykroyd and a multimillion dollar budget?

10. *Slapstick of Another Kind* (1983)—Jerry Lewis, Madeline Kahn and Marty Feldman star in this awful sci-fi spoof.

the B&W Channel saps them of their color and broadcasts them in black and white. "They seem funnier that way," says B&W spokesman Gil Moretti. Market studies have shown that "The Fresh Prince of Bel Air" actually generates more laughs in black and white than in color. But trouble looms for this channel before it's even launched: it's rumored that Ted Turner will buy the B&W channel and likely will colorize all its programming. However, directors such as Martin Scorsese and Tim Burton have vowed to fight Turner and what they call "a desecration of American television comedy."

SECURITYVISION

Ever wish you knew what went on in office building reception areas in Provo, Utah? Wonder what goes on in the lobby of that towering apartment building in downtown Boston? Now you can find out. When your cable system carries Securityvision, you will be connected, twenty-four hours a day, to a network of security cameras across America. "Hey, what's that guy doing with that suspicious-looking package in Chicago?" "Why did that woman go all the way up to the sixteenth floor of the Transamerica Tower? I think they might want to call the San Fran P.D. about her." With Securityvision, the eyes and ears of vigilant guards throughout the country are enhanced by you, the viewer. You can be a security guard from the safety of your own couch.

THE LECTURE HALL NETWORK

In the grand tradition of "Mystery Science Theater 3000" comes The Lecture Hall Network. If you've been to college, you've been forced to listen to professors drone on and on about molecular physics or the role of the United States in the Spanish-American War. What fun is that? Well, when

TOP COMEDIANS WHO'VE BEEN ANIMATED (NOT INCLUDING GUEST STARS ON "THE SIMPSONS")

- Louie Anderson—His own cartoon
- Robin Williams—*Aladdin*
- Jon Lovitz—The Critic
- Gilbert Gottfried—*Aladdin*
- Martin Short—Ed Grimley
- Dom Deluise—*All Dogs Go to Heaven*
- Joanne Worley—*Beauty and the Beast*
- Lily Tomlin—Edith Ann
- Howie Mandel—*Bobby's World*
- Morey Amsterdam—*Rudolph's Shiny New Year*

you watch LHN, you'll endure some of the deadliest lectures in colleges across America. But your traveling companions are Frankie Mosh, a guy from town, and his two beer-drinking robot buddies. Frankie went to community college for two weeks and thinks all the kids at the U are "real douchebags for goin' to school," so he sits in the back of lecture halls at colleges all over the country with you and comments on everything from the professor's tie to the physical attributes of the students in the class. Frankie and his pals are going down and they're taking you with them. Think of it as flunking out of college with three of your funniest friends.

*   *   *

Television isn't the only place that the comedy onslaught will be felt. The explosion of CD-ROM technology has made accessing information as easy for the novice as it has been for the expert. Here are some we can expect to see over the next few years.

EVERYTHING STEVE ALLEN'S EVER WRITTEN

Just what the title says: every song, book, sketch, essay, lecture, shopping list, condolence note and signed report card in the Allen oeuvre. Advanced CD-ROM programming includes full-motion video of Steve and his wife, Jayne Meadows, recalling where and when Steve wrote everything. And the entire text is cross-referenced, based on the words *I, me,* and *Steve.*

TIRADES: JERRY, UNDONE

Jerry Lewis himself takes you through an audio/video history of his most memorable rants. Click on the icon of the throbbing vein and watch Jerry berate a studio executive for the lousy marketing of *Hardly Working.* The tiny icon that resembles a bottle of painkillers takes you to Jerry, adrift in a fog of Percodans at the 1983 telethon, raging at bandleader Lou Brown for missing a cue. And the button with the image of the displaced family transports you to a scene of Jerry playing with his tiny daughter Danielle, while he browbeats washed-up, middle-aged rocker son Gary over the speakerphone. For every CD-ROM sold, a small sick child will get a brief visit from Jerry and a photographer, during which Jerry will refer to the photog as "Scavullo" and to the child as "the little cocker." Truly a worthy cause.

UNCLE MILTIE'S BEDTIME STORIES

A collection of reminiscences designed to lull you to sleep from Mr. Television himself, Milton Berle. Everyone's favorite uncle transports users to dreamland with meandering tales of his boyhood in vaudeville and his days as a television pioneer. Adding to the CD's authenticity: the video is in grainy black and white and filled with atmospheric scratches and dirt and Uncle Miltie often loses his way in the stories, leaving gaps that help soothe the user to sleep.

GET ME TO THE CLUB ON TIME!

An interactive game where you have to keep second-rate comic Joey Yocks from getting to the Bust-A-Gut comedy club in time for his performance that evening. You are Bobby Bits, a comic who'll stop at nothing to get a shot at the Bust-A-Gut, even if it means planting illegal drugs in Joey's condo, then calling the cops. You've won when Morty, the club's owner, discovers Joey in bed with Morty's teenage daughter. A fight ensues, gunfire erupts and Joey takes one in the gut. Morty, not wanting to lose a night's business, hires you to go on in Joey's place, ensuring stardom for you and obscurity for your rival.

Television and computers won't be the only media affected, of course. Clubs and live performers will also take advantage of new technologies.

GOGGLES AND GIGGLES: THE FIRST VIRTUAL COMEDY CLUB

Located in malls and amusement centers around the country, Goggles and Giggles is the first comedy club where anybody can be a comedian. At the door, the user pays five dollars for five minutes of "stage" time. He steps up on a platform and dons the goggles, through which he sees what a nightclub comic would: a room full of hostile drunks waiting for him to make them laugh. The goggles also display a teleprompter full of jokes for the "comic" to try. The bit can go one of two ways: either the user kills and the crowd loves him. Or, as more often happens, he bombs and the goggles slowly start to emit beads of flop sweat (made from the sweat of actual second-rate comics). The crowd becomes more and more nasty until the club owner throws you bodily (in a virtual way) out the door of the club and into the alley. Each Goggles and Giggles amusement center will have a genuine liquor license, so that fake comics who don't make the cut can do what real ones do: tie one on.

By now, Andy Warhol's observation that everyone will be famous for fifteen minutes is a bit of a cliché. But if any of the ideas that we've discussed make it off the drawing board, Warhol's prediction will be that much closer to reality. And isn't it frightening to think that your pot-bellied neighbor, the one who insists on mowing his lawn shirtless, might one day have his own television series? It could happen.